QuickBooks Tutorials

By Peterson

Table of Contents

QuickBooks Tutorials. 1 1
By Peterson.. 1 1
Table of Contents. 2 2
Introduction.. 5 7
Start QuickBooks. 5 7
Chart of Accounts. 7 10
Balance Sheet Accounts. 7 10
Income and expense accounts. 8 11
Cost of goods sold (COGS) account8 12
Customers and Vendors. 12 17
Add a customer. 12 17
Add vendors. 13 19
A customer who is also a vendor. 15 20
Merge two vendor names. 15 21
Setting up items. 17 22
Benefits of setting up items. 17 22
Types of QuickBooks items. 18 23
Items that calculate. 18 24
Setting up your items with different units of measure. 20 27
Setting up different units of measure. 22 29
Adding items with units of measure to forms. 22 30
Reporting in different units of measure. 23 31
Items to subtotal on sales forms. 24 33
Entering a group of items. 25 34
To create a group item:25 34
To remove an item from a group:26 35
Applying a discount to one or more items. 26 35
Payment item.. 26 36
Adjusting opening balances for balance sheet accounts. 28 ... 39
Check the quantity of an inventory item.. 29 40
Adjust the quantity of an inventory item.. 29 40
Purchase Forms. 31 42

Purchase order. 31 42
Enter Bills and Pay bills. 37 51
Enter a bill for expenses. 39 54
Apply credit from a vendor to a bill payment41 57
Apply a discount to a bill you pay. 42 58
Enter a bill against an item receipt43 59
Return items after you've entered a bill43 60
To apply credit from a vendor to a bill payment44 61
Sales Forms. 46..63
Invoices. 46..63
Create a recurring invoice. 47..65
Manage your memorized transactions. 49 68
Void an invoice. 51..71
Delete an invoice. 52 72
Record a partial payment using a payment item.. 52.............72
Receive payments. 52 73
Discount and Credits. 53 74
Enter Sales Receipts. 57 81
Credit memos. 59...85
Use a customer credit as payment60 87
Statements. 62..89
Estimate. 63 92
Create an invoice from an estimate. 65 94
Bad debts. 67 96
Fixed Assets. 71...101
To record a purchase of a fixed asset71 101
Buy fixed assets for your business. 73 103
To enter a fixed asset bought with personal funds. 73 104
To transfer a fixed asset from your personal holdings to your business. 74..105
Record thefts or losses of fixed assets. 74 106
Sell an asset75 107
Handling Pre-Paid Expenses. 78 111
Sales tax. 79 113
QuickBooks sales tax terminology. 81 115
Set up sales tax. 82 117
Sales tax codes. 83 119
Sales tax payment schedule. 84......................................120
Pay sales tax. 85..122

Manufacturing Firm Inventory. 87 125
Reconcile a Bank Account. 92 130
Adding Users in QuickBooks and Giving Them Access. 96 134
Practice Exercise.. 100..138

Introduction

This tutorial furthers the learner's knowledge of Intuit QuickBooks application. QuickBooks is bookkeeping software created and marketed by Intuit and its one of the most popular accounting and book keeping programs available today.

QuickBooks is a terrific program to learn, as the skills that you learn in QuickBooks can save valuable time and money by automating, organizing and structuring the book keeping of your company.

QuickBooks allows you track inventory, create invoices, create customer statements, pay your bills, write checks as well as perform accounting and business related tasks.

Start QuickBooks

i. Click on the Start button on the Task Bar
ii. Choose All Programs from the Start menu
iii. Choose QuickBooks from the Program menu
iv. Click on QuickBooks Pro Edition from the menu

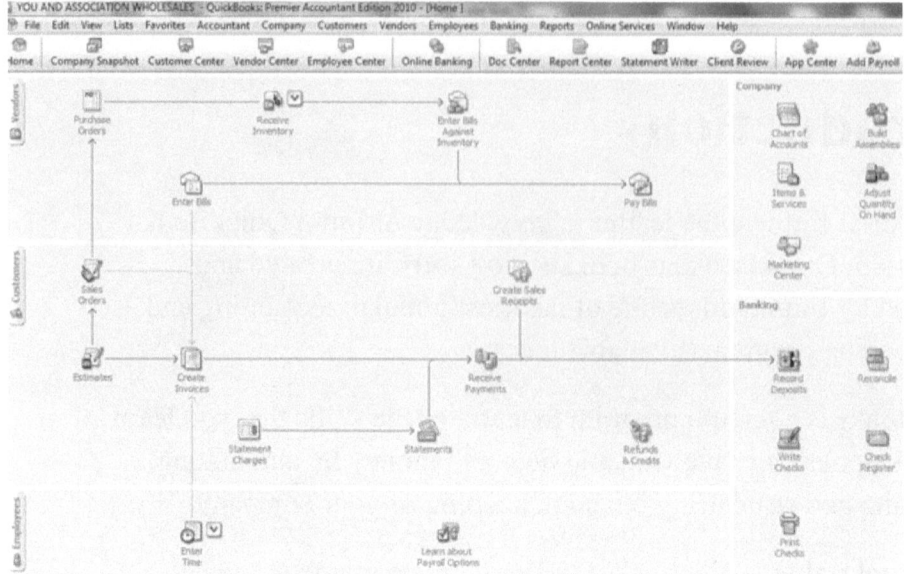

You can also use the program's menu bar and ribbon to choose commands you will need to work with the open company file. To use the menu bar, click an option on the menu bar, such as Reports. Choose an option from the drop-down list, such as Company & Financial. Some of the options on the drop-down lists have an arrow on the right side which indicates that additional choices are available under these options. For example, several reports are listed under the Company & Financial option.

Reports	Online Services	Window	Help					
Report Center								
Company Snapshot			p Center	Add Payroll	Cards & eChecks	Services		
Memorized Reports	▶							
Process Multiple Reports				QuickBook				
Intuit Statement Writer								
Company & Financial	▶	Profit & Loss Standard						
Customers & Receivables	▶	Profit & Loss Detail						
Sales	▶	Profit & Loss YTD Comparison						
Jobs, Time & Mileage	▶	Profit & Loss Prev Year Comparison						
Vendors & Payables	▶	Profit & Loss by Job						
Purchases	▶	Profit & Loss by Class						
Inventory	▶	Profit & Loss Unclassified						
Employees & Payroll	▶	Income by Customer Summary						
Banking	▶	Income by Customer Detail						
Accountant & Taxes	▶	Expenses by Vendor Summary						
Budgets & Forecasts	▶	Expenses by Vendor Detail						
List	▶	Income & Expense Graph						
Industry Specific	▶							
		Balance Sheet Standard						
Custom Summary Report		Balance Sheet Detail						
Custom Transaction Detail Report		Balance Sheet Summary						
		Balance Sheet Prev Year Comparison						
QuickReport	Ctrl+Q	Net Worth Graph						
Transaction History								
Transaction Journal		Statement of Cash Flows						

Chart of Accounts

One of the first steps in setting up a new accounting system is the creation of a chart of accounts, which is simply a list of named accounts that the company expects to use for recording and reporting financial transactions. It shows a balance for each balance sheet account.

The list of its accounts has the following:
   a. Balance sheet accounts
   b. Income accounts
   c. Expense accounts
   d. Cost of goods sold accounts
   e. Non-posting accounts which includes purchase orders and estimates, which don't appear on your balance sheet

Some of these accounts are created for you automatically. For example, the first time you create an invoice or statement charge, QuickBooks automatically creates an accounts receivable account. You'll add other accounts during setup using the Easy Step Interview. You can create and modify your accounts as needed at any time.

Balance Sheet Accounts

Your chart of accounts includes balance sheet accounts. These accounts track the following:
   a. What you have, known as assets
   b. What people owe you, known accounts receivable
   c. What your company owes to other people, known as accounts payable and other liabilities
   d. The net worth of your company, known as equity

Account types

   a. **Bank;** Transactions in checking, savings, petty cash and money market accounts

b. **Accounts Receivable;** Transactions between company and its customers. This includes invoices, statement charges, payments from customers, deposits of customer payments, refunds, and credit memos. QuickBooks automatically creates this account when you first create an invoice or statement charge
c. **Other Current Asset;** Assets that are likely to be converted to cash or used up within a period of one year e.g. the value of your inventory on hand, prepaid expenses
d. **Fixed Asset;** Depreciable assets that aren't liquid (not likely to be converted into cash within a year), e.g. equipment, furniture
e. **Other Asset;** Any asset that is neither a current asset nor a fixed asset, such as long-term notes receivable
f. **Accounts Payable (A/P);** Outstanding bills. When you first enter a bill, QuickBooks automatically creates an A/P account
g. **Other Current Liability;** Liabilities that are scheduled to be paid within one year, such as sales tax, payroll taxes, accrued or deferred salaries, and short-term loans. Some businesses include the current portion of long-term liabilities in this kind of account

Income and expense accounts

Income and expense accounts track the sources of income and the purpose of each expense. When you record transactions in a balance sheet account, you usually assign the amount of the transaction to one or more income or expense accounts. For example, you not only record that you took money out of your bank account, but you keep track of what you spent the money on, such as rent, advertising, office supplies, fuel.

QuickBooks has no registers for income and expense accounts, but you can create reports to show totals for these accounts over a period of time.

Cost of goods sold (COGS) account

Many businesses that track inventory have one cost of goods sold account, which is similar to an expense account. A COGS account contains the cost of inventory you have sold.

Add an account on chart of accounts

You add new accounts as your business grows and changes.
    i.   Choose List, then Chart of Accounts

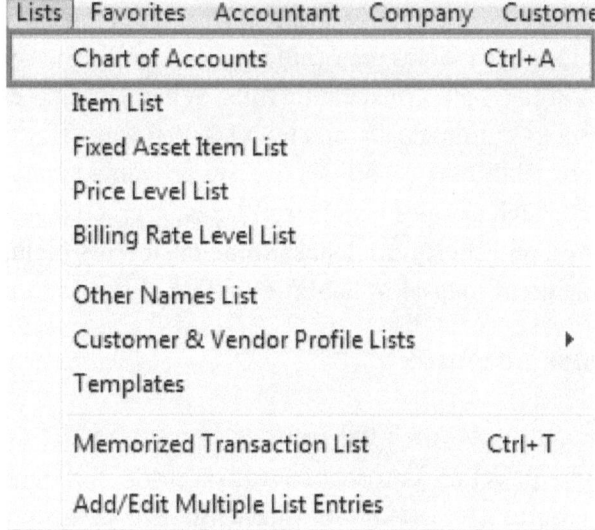

QuickBooks displays Chart of accounts window.
    ii.   Choose account, then click New at the bottom of the window

- Payroll Expenses
- Postage and Delivery
- Professional Fees
- Rent Expense
- Repairs and Maintenance
- Telephone Expense
- Travel Expense
- Utilities
- Finance Charge Income

[Account ▼] [Activities ▼] [Reports ▼] [Attach] [ ] Include inactive

QuickBooks displays the first Add New account window.

iii. Identify the type of the account that you are adding
QuickBooks supplies a number of account types. They tell the QuickBooks which areas of the financial statement account data gets reported

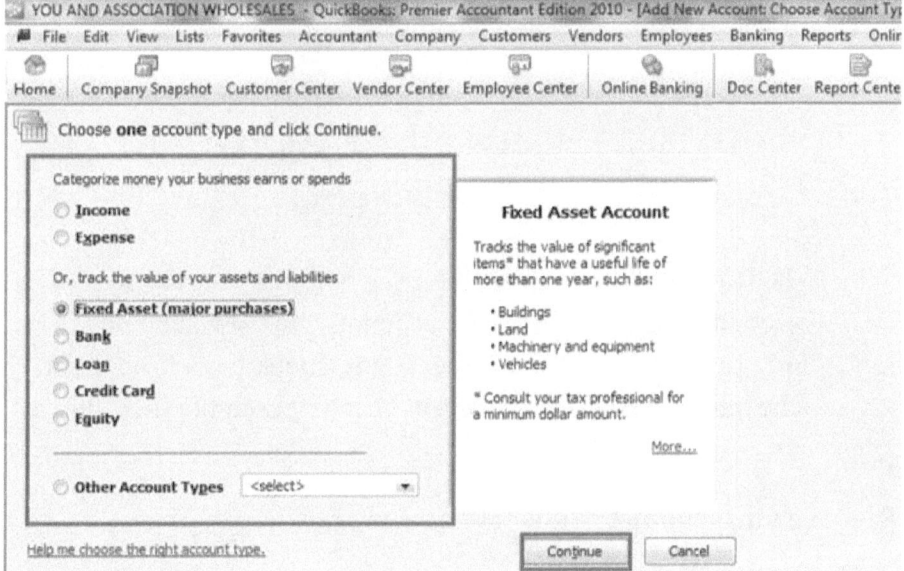

iv. Click continue

QuickBooks displays the add new account window

v. Use the name box to give the new account a unique name. The name will appear on the financial statements

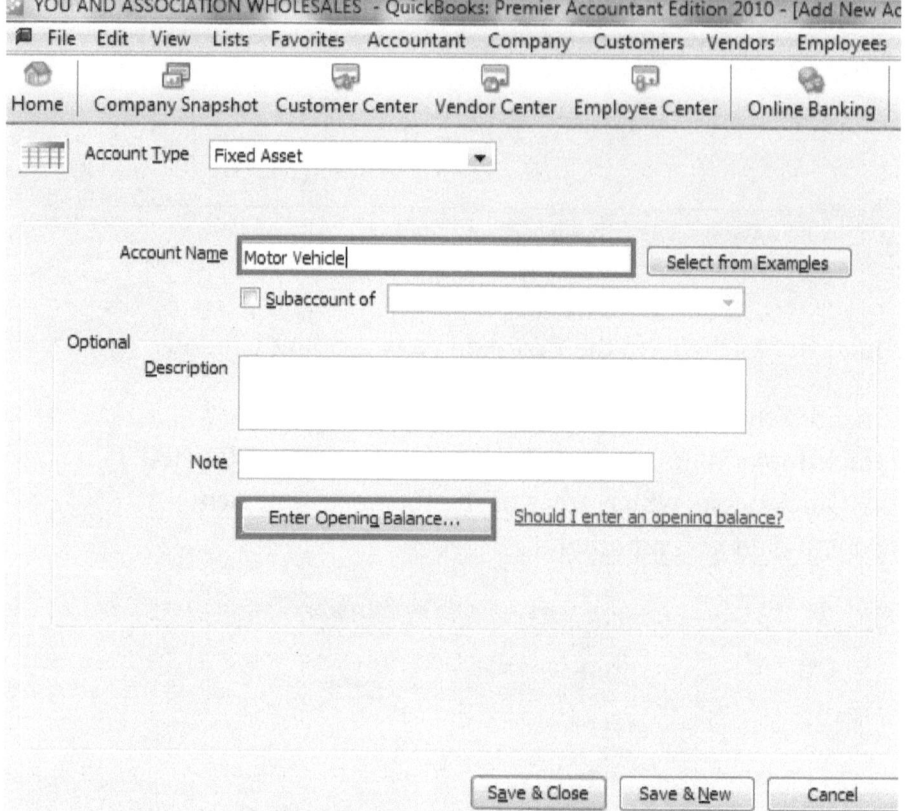

vi. If the account you are adding is a sub-account of a parent account, indicate the parent account, click save and new. On the name box enter the sub account, check the sub account checkbox and select the parent account from the drop down list

Remove an account or subaccount

There are three ways to remove an account from your Chart of Accounts:

a. **Combine (merge) two accounts**
Say you have both an Office Supplies account and a Business Supplies account. You might want to merge the two accounts so you can see the transactions for both accounts listed as a single line in your reports

b. **Hide an account (by making it inactive)**
Because you don't want to lose historical transactions, you don't want to delete an account that you aren't using anymore. It's better to hide the account in your chart of accounts by making it inactive

c. **Delete an account**
Unless you've set up an account by mistake, it's better for your records to hide an account instead of deleting it. There are limitations when you delete an account

Combine two accounts

i. Click the Lists menu, and then click Chart of Accounts
ii. Make sure the two accounts you want to merge are at the same hierarchical level on the list. If they're at different levels, move one account to the same level as the other. To do this:

   a. Move the mouse to the small diamond at the left of the account name. When the mouse pointer touches the diamond, the pointer changes to a four-headed arrow to indicate that you can drag the account to a new position in the chart of accounts

   b. Click and drag the diamond to the left or right until the account is indented the same amount as the account that you want to merge it with

iii. Click the account you don't want to use

iv. Click Account at the bottom of the list and click Edit Account

v. Change the account name so that it matches the account you're merging it with

vi. Click OK

vii. To merge the two accounts click Yes

Customers and Vendors

A customer is any person or company who pays for goods or services you offer. QuickBooks uses Customer Center to hold information about customers. Vendors are any person or company that you purchase goods or services from. QuickBooks uses the Vendors list to hold information about the vendors.

Add a customer

   a. Click Customer Center

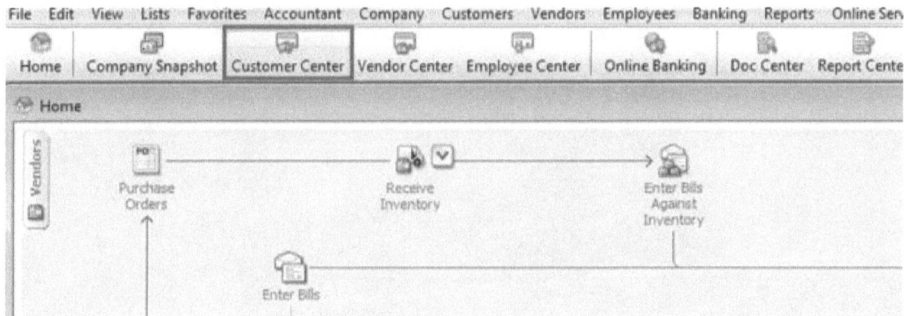

   b. Click New Customer & Job at the top of the Customer Center and then click New Customer

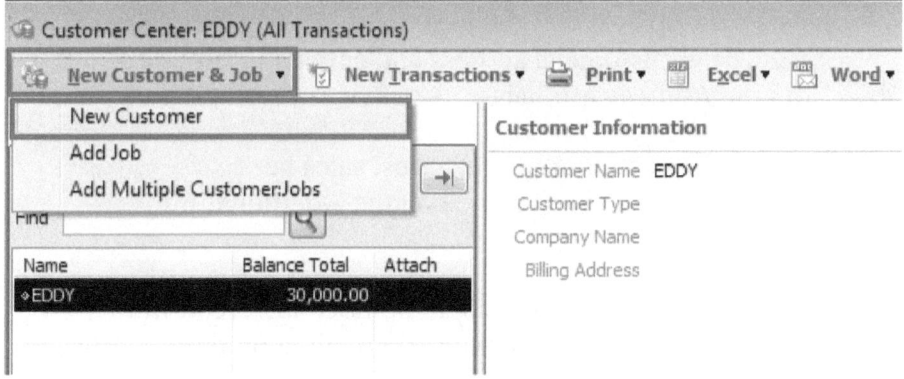

   c. In the Customer Name field, enter the name of the customer as you'd like it to appear in your Customers & Jobs list

d. If you have an outstanding balance for this customer, enter the Opening balance and "as of" information

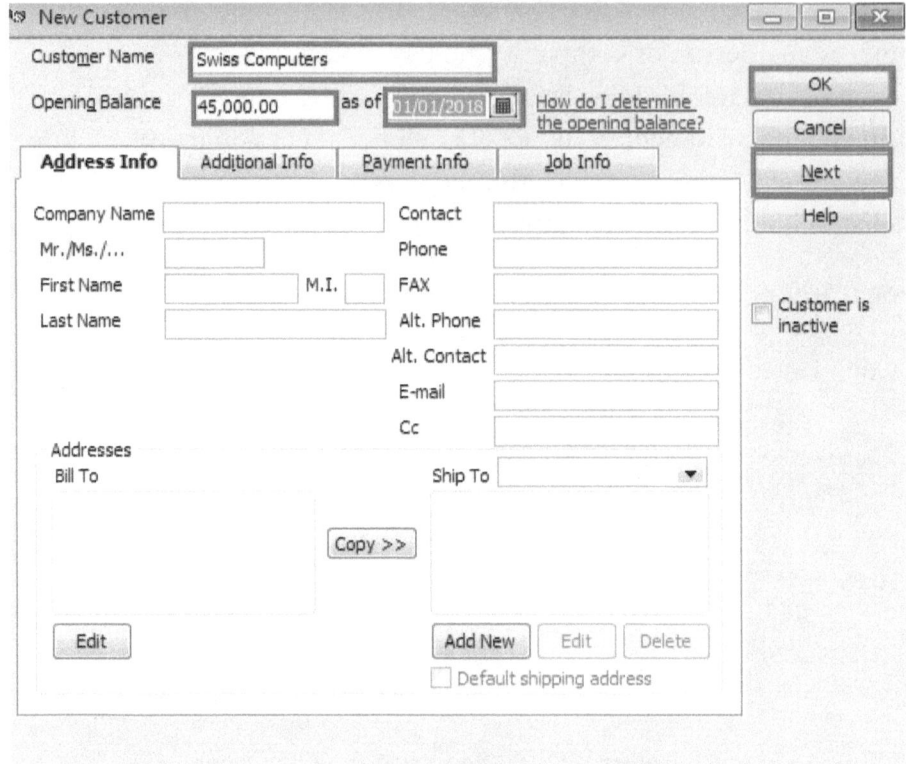

e. Add other details about the customer

    a. Enter the customer's address and contact information on the Address Info tab.

    b. Enter the customer's type, terms, sales tax information, and price level on the Additional Info tab

    c. Enter the customer's account number and credit limit, as well as the preferred payment method on the Payment Info tab

f. Click Next to save the customer information and enter another customer name. Click OK to save the customer information and close the window

Add vendors

To add a vendor:

i. Click Vendor Center

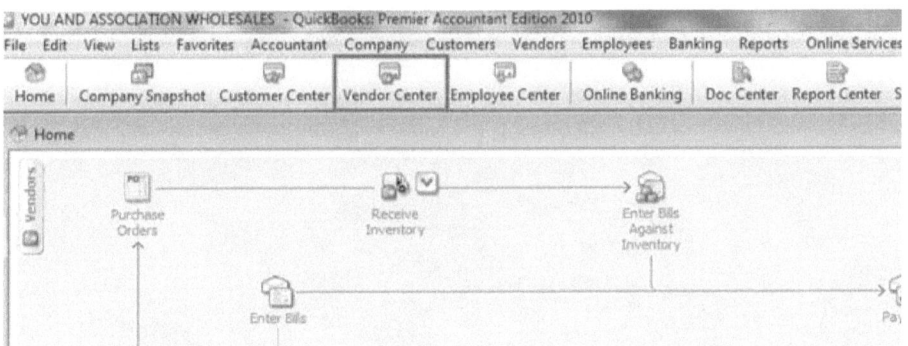

ii. Click New Vendor

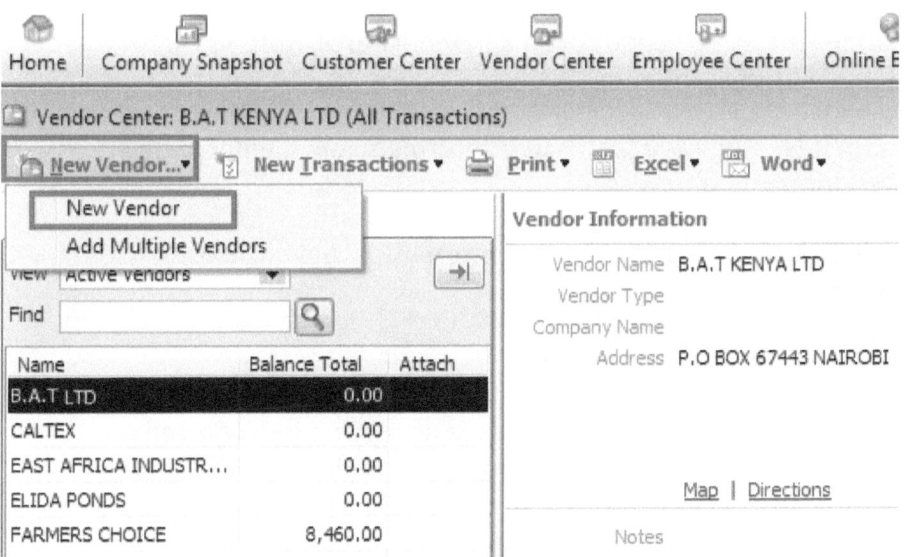

iii. In the Vendor Name field, enter the name of the vendor

iv. If you have an outstanding balance for money that you owe to this vendor, enter the Opening Balance and "as of" information

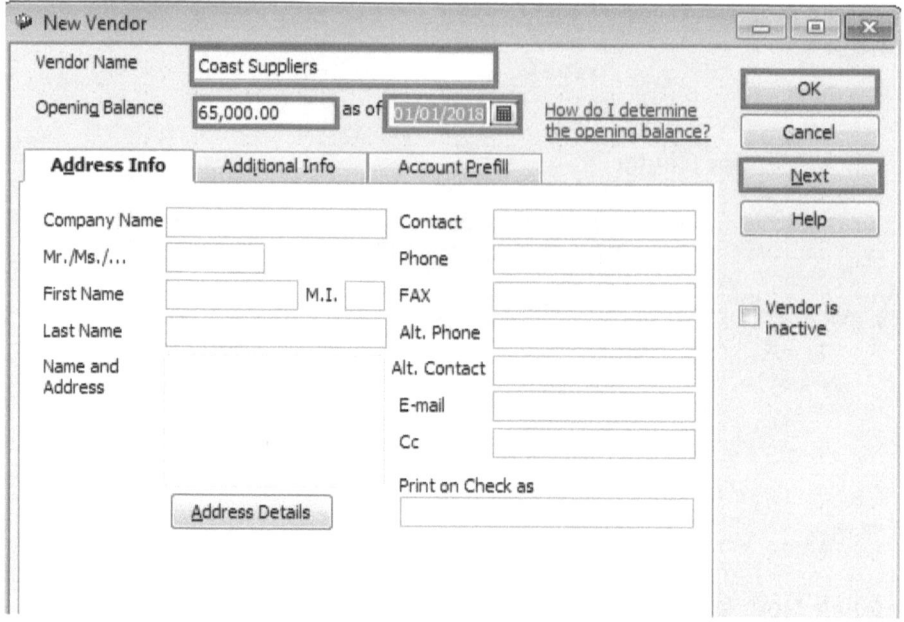

v. Enter the other vendor details in the Address Info tab and the Additional Info tab

vi. Click Next to save the vendor information and enter another vendor name if necessary

vii. Click OK to save the vendor information and close the window

A customer who is also a vendor

If you do business with a customer who is also a vendor (or a vendor who is also a customer), add the person's name to both your customer and vendor lists, but vary the name slightly or tag the name with an identifying letter or number. For example, if you have a vendor named Wayne tech, you might list the name as Wayne tech _C (for customer) in your customer list and Wayne tech _V (for vendor) in your vendor list.

To make sure that the same real name will print on any invoices or checks for this person, enter the person's real name in the "Bill to" field for customers and in the "Print on Check as" field for vendors. Find these fields are at the bottom of the Address Info tab in the New Customer and New Vendor windows.

Merge two vendor names

To merge two vendor names:

i. Click the Vendor Center

ii. Click the Vendors tab

iii. Right-click the vendor name you don't want to use, and then click Edit Vendor

iv. In the Edit Vendor window, change the vendor name to the same name as the vendor you're combining it with

v. Click OK

vi. Click Yes to confirm that you want to merge the two vendor names under the same name

Once you merge two vendor names, you can't reverse it. All transactions, even in closed periods, will be under the one name. It may also affect previous financial reports. The data associated with the merged vendor, such as address, phone number, etc., is removed from your records along with the name.

Setting up items

This section is about adding items to QuickBooks. You can add items at any time as part of setting up QuickBooks or whenever you think of an item you need to use.

Remember, items are for the services or items you buy and sell. You also may need special calculating items that calculate subtotals and discounts, and that apply specific sales tax rates.

The EasyStep Interview helps you set up a few items, so you may already have some items.

Fixed asset items are not set up in the EasyStep Interview.

Benefits of setting up items

i. You can use sales forms in QuickBooks to track the details of how your business earns its income. Estimates and all sales forms (invoices, sales receipts, and credit memos) require items. So do QuickBooks statement charges, which print on statements

ii. You can fill out sales forms or enter statement charges quickly. QuickBooks automatically enters the description and rate or price you entered in the item's setup window. When you enter a quantity, QuickBooks calculates the amount

iii. When you record a sale, QuickBooks automatically tracks the income in the appropriate income account. You can fill out a sales form, keep track of your sales, and keep track of income all in one step

iv. You can create reports that show total units of each service or product sold as well as amount totals

QuickBooks stores information about your items on the Item list. When you set up most items, you must specify which account it should affect when you use the item on a sale or purchase. Then, when you record the sale or purchase, each item on it affects the appropriate account.

In other words, while you are recording the items on a sale or purchase, QuickBooks is adjusting all the right accounts behind the scenes.

Information about fixed assets is available in the Fixed Asset Item List. The Fixed Asset Item
List is only available in QuickBooks Pro and better.

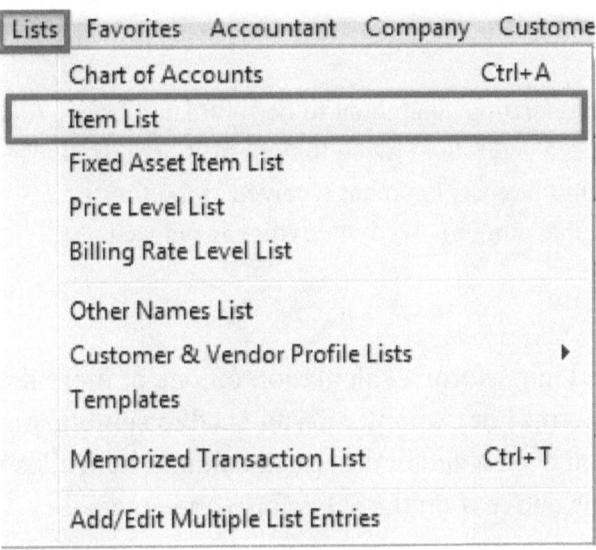

Types of QuickBooks items

A part from items for services or products, QuickBooks has several other types of items:
   a. **Service;** used for Services you charge for or services you purchase Examples: professional fees, labor
   b. **Inventory Part;** Products you purchase, track as inventory, then resell
   c. **Inventory Assembly;** Assembled products you purchase or create and build, track as inventory, then resell
   d. **Non-inventory Part;** Products you sell but don't purchase; items you purchase and resell but do not track as inventory; items you enter on purchase orders

e. **Fixed Asset;** Property that will contribute to the operating capacity of your company for several years E.g: Vehicles, Computers, machinery
f. **Other Charge;** Other charges on a sale or a purchase e.g: Shipping charge, delivery charge, finance charge
g. **Subtotal;** Calculating and printing a subtotal on sales forms
h. **Group;** Fast entry of a group of individual items already on the list Example: A group of services and food items provided by a caterer
i. **Discount;** Calculating an amount to be subtracted from a total or subtotal E.g: A 5% discount given to nonprofit organizations
j. **Payment;** On invoices: Payment received at the time of invoicing, so that amount owed on invoice is reduced

Items that calculate

These items are used to perform a calculation on one or more lines above it on a sales form. For example, if you need to subtotal on sales forms, then you need a subtotal item. A subtotal item adds the amounts of the items above it on the sales form and enters the subtotal on the form.

Finally, there are some items that can be set up either as percentages or with flat amounts, depending on what you need. For example, Charles adds a 10 % service charge to her invoices.
He has set up an other charge item with a rate of 10 %. He uses a subtotal item before the service charge, so that the 10 % will be based on the subtotal amount.
Mary gives a 15 % discount to certain customers. She has set up a discount item with a rate of 15 %. She must use a subtotal item, because the discount is based on the entire amount.

Sub items

On your chart of accounts, you can have an item with related sub-items. For example, Charles keeps the books for his gift shop, which sells T-shirts and other items. He has an item called T-shirts and sub-items called Adult and Child, each with its own price.

It enables you to put similar items together on your Item list, so you can locate them easily on the drop-down list in any Item field. Each sub-item can have its own rate or price and its own description. Each sub-item can even have its own account, although you would probably assign the same account to all sub-items of the same parent item.

On reports based on items, QuickBooks subtotals each group of sub-items.

Group and inventory assembly items

They have a completely different purpose from sub-items.
Group and assembly items allow you to enter a group of items that is, several different items at once on a sale or purchase. Group items are appropriate for combining several types of items, such as food items. Assembly items, available only in QuickBooks, are appropriate for indicating products you combine and sell as a unit. Note that you can't group fixed assets or make them sub-items of other items.

Change an item's type

You can change an item's type if the item is a non-inventory part, an Other Charge item, or an inventory part. You can change:

a. An Other Charge item to a service, non-inventory part, inventory part, or an inventory assembly item

b. A non-inventory item to a service, Other Charge, inventory part, or inventory assembly item

c. An inventory part item to an inventory assembly item

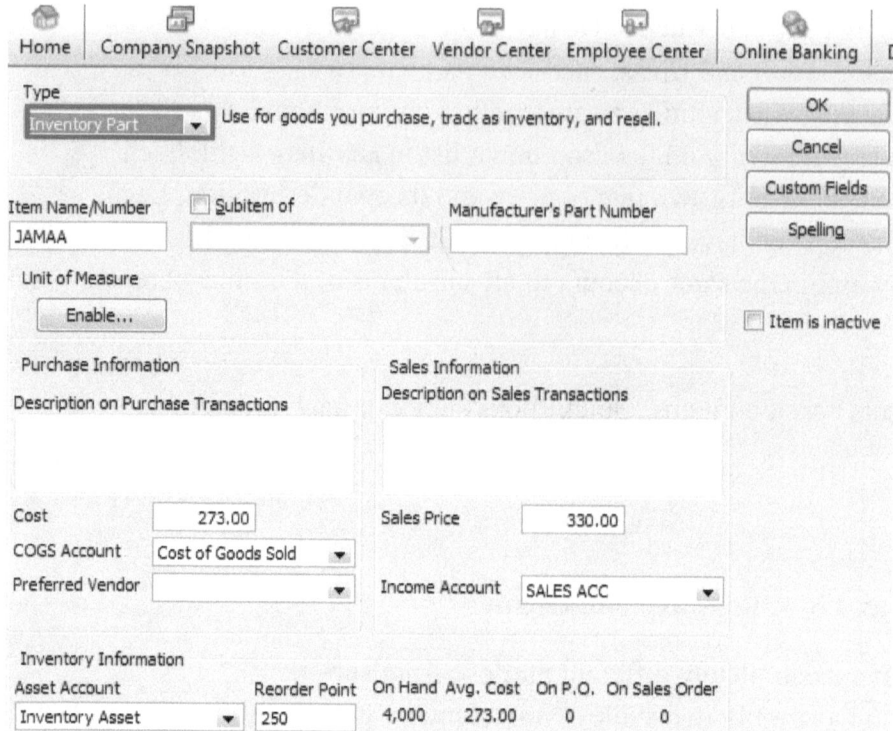

To do this task:

i. Go to the Lists menu and click Item List
ii. Double-click the item that you want to change
iii. Click the Type drop-down arrow and click the type you want
iv. Click OK

If you are changing the item to an inventory part or an inventory assembly item, the "as of" date that you enter for the total value of the item must be a date that is after the date of the last transaction that uses the item

Because the types of items that can be changed and what they can be changed to is limited, you cannot always "change an item back" if you change your mind. For example, if you change an Other Charge item to an inventory part item, you can no longer change its type

Setting up your items with different units of measure

A company can use different units of measure for inventory and inventory-assembly type items. You would set up items with different units of measure if you purchased in one unit (e.g. a crate), but sold that item using another unit (e.g. can). For example, you can buy soda in crates with 12 cans to a crate, and sell the by the can. Then, when you sell one can, QuickBooks understands this transaction to mean 1/12 of your inventory.

Turning on the units of measure preference

Note that the units of measure preference cannot be turned off once it has been enabled. You should only consider activating this preference if you buy stock or sell in different units.
Before setting up different units of measure for items, the units of measure preference must be turned on.

    i.   From the Edit menu, choose Preferences

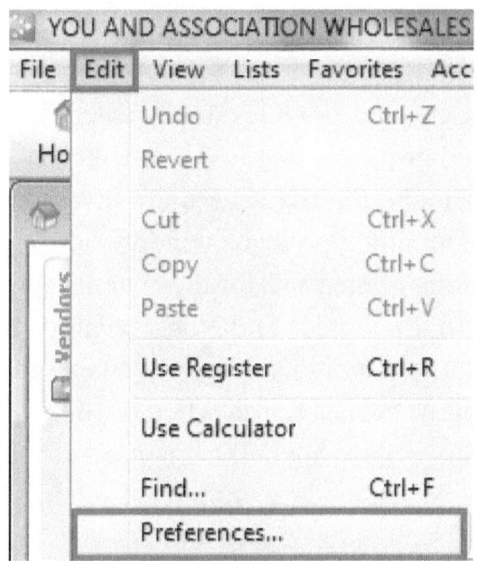

    ii.   From the scroll box on the left, select Items & Inventory

iii. On the Company Preferences tab, select Inventory and purchase orders are active, and then select Units of Measure are active. Inventory must be turned on in order to activate units of measure

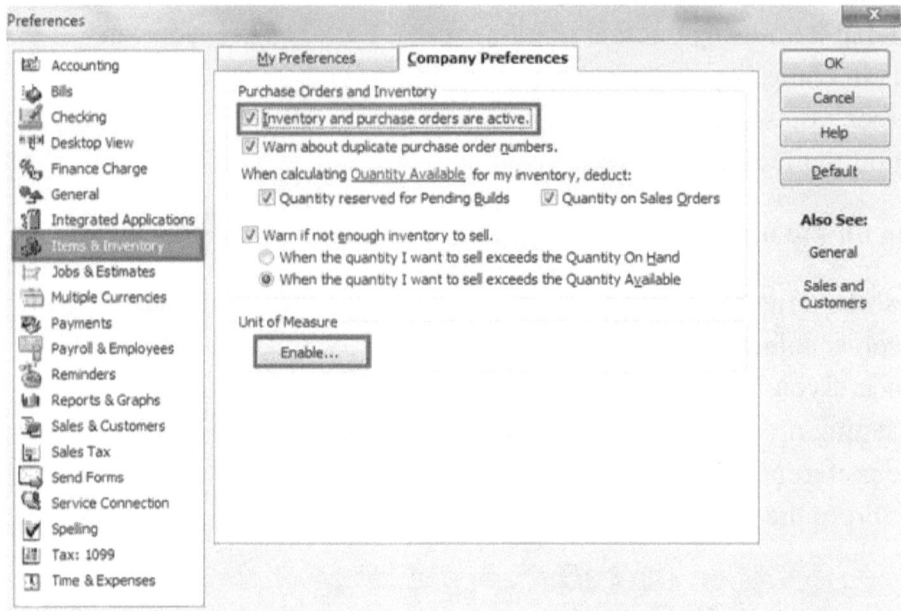

You'll see the following changes in QuickBooks when the units of measure preference turned on:
    a. A Units of Measure button is added to the Inventory Part and Inventory Assembly type items window where you can set up different units of measure for these items
    b. A field is added to the Service and Non-inventory Part items window where you can assign a descriptive label that represents the unit of measure used when dealing with the item. Note that this in only a label that is used as a descriptor on various forms. When dealing with Service items, you cannot define different units of measure
    c. A Unit column is added to all forms to display the item's unit of measure associated with the type of transaction. Selling unit is used on sales forms such as invoices and sales

orders, and the purchasing unit on purchase forms such as bills and purchase orders
- d. A Unit column is also displayed on Adjust Quantity/Value on Hand and Change Item Prices
- e. A Unit column is added to display an item's units of measure on reports to do with the item list; and purchases, sales and inventory transactions

Setting up different units of measure

You can keep track of how you purchase, stock and sell your items with the units of measure preference turned on,. You can define different units of measure for Inventory Part and
Inventory Assembly items. The association between an item's units of measure cannot be changed once a transaction involving the item is recorded. You must first set up an item's units of measure before entering a quantity on hand.

- i. From the Lists menu, choose Item List
- ii. From the Item menu button, choose New
- iii. From the Type field of the New Item window, choose Inventory Part or Inventory Assembly, and then click the Units of Measure button. The Define Units of Measure window appears

For items that are already in your inventory, you must set up the units of measure on the Define Units of Measure window before you enter a Quantity on Hand on the New Item Window. Once you enter a quantity on hand for a new item, you cannot change its units of measure.

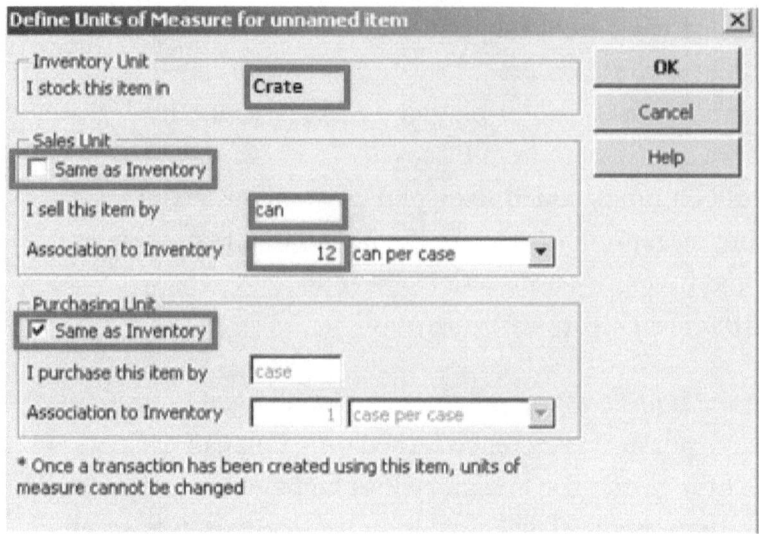

iv. Under the "I stock this item in" text box, type the unit of measure you use to stock the item

v. Clear "Same as Inventory " check- box and type the unit you use when selling the item

vi. Enter the number of selling units that make up a stocking unit under the "Association to Inventory" text box

vii. Keep the "Same as Inventory" check box checked if the purchasing unit is the same as the stocking unit. If the purchasing unit is different, clear the box

viii. Click OK, and continue setting up the item

Adding items with units of measure to forms

Once units of measure are set up for an item, the item's appropriate unit of measure is then displayed on business forms. Sales forms show the selling units, and purchasing forms show purchasing units. On forms, you cannot switch to a different unit of measure.

On Bills

An item's purchasing unit is shown when entering a bill. From the example shown above, the purchasing unit for Soda Pop is a crate. QuickBooks understands this to mean 12 cans as defined by the item's selling units of measure.

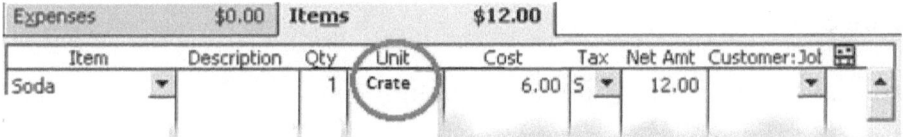

On Invoices

When that same item is shown on an invoice, the unit displayed is the selling unit.

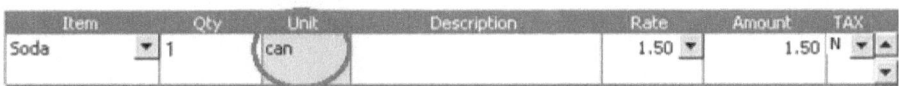

Fractional or decimal values can work on forms. E.g. for a half a case, you could enter .5 or 1/2 on your bill.

Reporting in different units of measure

Some reports display an item's unit of measure by default. The unit that is displayed depends on the report being created for a "Purchase by Item Summary" report displays the purchasing units of measure, whereas the "Sales by Item Summary" report displays the selling units. You can change the reports to display in the units you want through the Modify Report window.

0.08333

Adding items to Item list

QuickBooks has several different item types.

Item Type

After you choose the item type e.g. service type, inventory type, enter only the information it required for that particular item type. A fixed asset items cannot be created from this item list but you can use the Fixed Asset Item list to do it.

Item name/code

This is displayed on reports of items and in the drop-down list in the Item field.

Item description

Shows the entire description in the Description field of sales or purchase forms. This is optional on all but required on fixed assets.

Rate or price

Shows the rate or price in the Rate or Price fields of sales or purchase forms. Some items types can have a rate that is a percentage. This information is optional.

Account or accounts

Profit and loss statements report on the income or expense account associated with items used in transactions. Some types of items have separate accounts for sales and for purchases. Payment items require a balance sheet account instead of an income or expense account. Inventory items require three separate accounts.

Sub-item status

This is used if you want to make an item a sub-item of an existing item. QuickBooks displays Sub-items of the same item together.

Custom fields

These are fields that fill your company's needs. You can also customize sales and purchase forms to display a column for a custom field.

Items to subtotal on sales forms

The subtotal item adds up the amounts of the items above it, up to the last subtotal.
You'll need a subtotal item if you ever want to apply a percentage discount or a charge to several items.

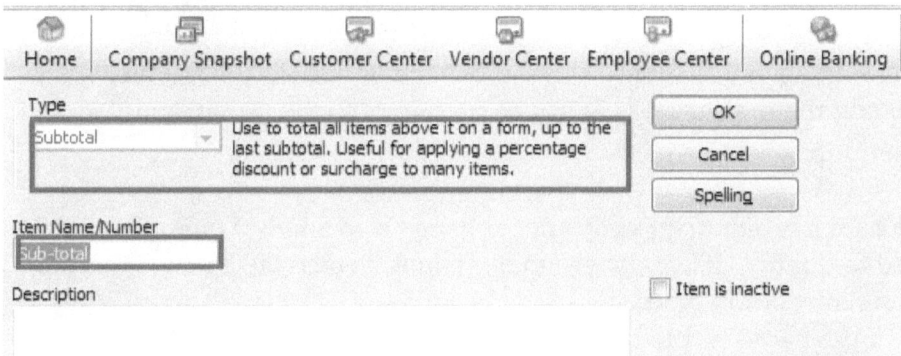

You'll need to subtotal the items before entering the percentage line item because QuickBooks calculates percentages on the line above. In case of two subtotals in a row, the last subtotal will add up all the previous subtotals on the form.

The first subtotal shows subtotal for the first two items (1600) while the second one shows the subtotal for the next three items (1670). The third subtotal adds up the two previous subtotals (3270).

Entering a group of items

The group item allows you to enter several items all at once on a sales form, estimate, purchase order, cheque, or bill. If you often sell the same group of items together, using a group item saves you the trouble of entering the same set of line items again and again.

When you use a group item, you can enter a quantity for the group that affects the quantity and amount of each item in the group. You can also edit the individual quantity of each item in the group, and edit descriptions and rates.

If you create a group item, you cannot change it to another type. If you need to do this, delete the group item, and then create a new item using the correct type.

To create a group item:
  i. On the Lists menu and click Item List
  ii. Click Item at the bottom of the list and click New
  iii. Click the Type drop-down arrow and then click Group
  iv. In the Group Name/Number field, enter a name or number for the group item
  v. Assign a unit of measure if unit of measure is available. This is optional
  vi. Enter a Description of the group item

   This description appears on sales forms.

vii. Select the Print items in group checkbox if you want your customers to see a list of the individual items and their amounts on your printed forms

Sub-items of an item in a group will not appear on printed forms. Leave the checkbox unselected if you don't want the details of the group to appear on your printed forms.

viii. In the Item column, select the items that you want to include in this group. You can include a maximum of 20 items in a group

ix. In the Qty column, enter the quantity that you want QuickBooks to enter for each individual item when you use the group item on a form

If you do not enter quantities, QuickBooks assumes that the quantity of each item is 1. You can always change the quantities when you enter a sale or purchase.

x. Click Custom Fields to fill in all custom fields that apply to this item

xi. Record the item

To remove an item from a group:

i. Go to the Lists menu and click Item List

ii. Double-click the group item

iii. Click the item within the group you want to delete, and then click Ctrl-Del

Applying a discount to one or more items

A discountrefers to a fixed amount or percentage that you deduct from the amount you charge a customer. To apply a discount, you have to enter a discount item. You cannot change it to another type once you create it. If the discount item's rate is a percentage, the item reduces the amount due by a percentage of the line above it. To take a percentage off several items at once, you must first subtotal the items. On the other hand, if you want to discount one particular item you've sold and not the entire sale, add a discount item directly beneath the one discounted item.

If you give discounts of different percentages, you can either set up a separate discount item for each percentage or edit the amount right on the sales form. Don't use a discount item for discounts that you give for early payment. Enter discounts for early payment through the Receive Payments window.

Payment item

You will need to enter a payment item if you receive a partial payment toward the amount of an invoice at the time you create the invoice.

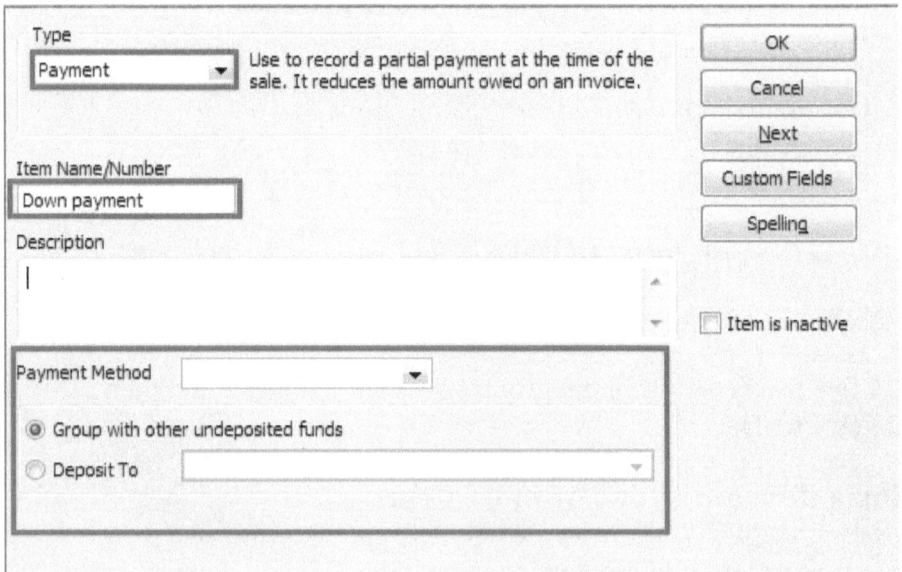

This item tells QuickBooks to subtract the amount of the payment from the total invoice amount. To record the payment on the invoice, enter a payment item for the amount you've received after you've entered all the items sold.

If you receive full payment at the time of the sale, use a sales receipt form instead of an invoice with a payment item. If you receive full or partial payment on an invoice or statement after you created it, enter the payment in the Receive Payments window.

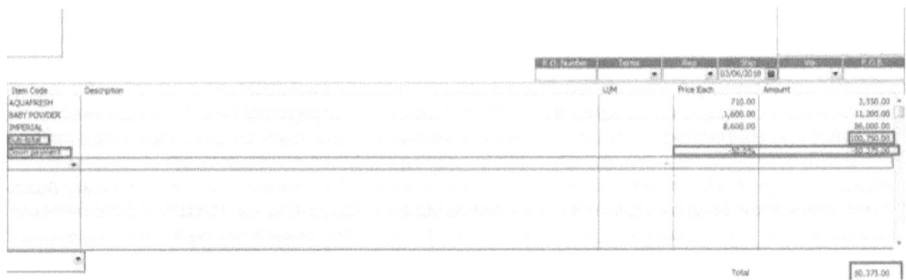

QuickBooks subtracts a payment item from the total amount on the invoice.

You can set up a payment item so that it automatically deposits the payment directly to a chequing or other account. On the other hand, you can set it up so that QuickBooks automatically puts the payment amount into your Undeposited Funds account so you can deposit it with other funds.

If you need to track the payment method (cheque, cash, credit card charge), you can have different payment items for different methods of payment.

Other ways to record a payment are:
    a. For partial payment received at time of sale, enter payment item on invoice
    b. For full payment received at time of sale, use sales receipt. Payment item is not necessary because QuickBooks records the sale as fully paid
    c. For payment from customer to pay outstanding invoice or statement, enter payment in Receive Payments window and

indicate which invoices or statement charges have been paid by the payment
d. For advance payment from customer, enter payment in Receive Payments window. Leave the credit to be used later or refund the amount. In case you have an invoice for this customer, you can apply the down payment amount

Hiding and redisplaying items on lists

You can hide an item on the Item or Fixed Asset Item list without deleting it by making the item inactive.

When you make an item inactive, QuickBooks keeps the information associated with that item, but hides the item on the Item list and removes it from any drop-down lists that use items. You do not need to change or delete any transaction that uses the item. If you start to use the item again, you can make it active at any time.
You can display all your items, including the inactive ones, on the Item list by selecting Show All. Note that inactive items still appear on reports, but never display on drop-down lists.

Delete an entry from a list

Delete entries one at a time. You can't delete an entry if it has ever been used in a transaction, even if the transaction is completed. It makes for better bookkeeping records to hide the item in the list.

To do this task:

a. Go to the Lists menu and click the list that you want to delete an entry from, such as the Item List
b. Single-click the entry in the list. Be sure to only single-click the entry because if you double-click the entry, you'll open a window to edit it instead of deleting it
c. Go to the Edit menu and click Delete. The Delete command will contain the list name. E.g. to delete an entry from the Class List, you would select Delete Class. If the entry you

want to delete has been used in a transaction, you'll receive a message telling you that you can't delete it. You may want to hide the entry instead.

Note that the only time you can revert a deletion is immediately after you delete it. If you perform any other action in QuickBooks, you won't be able to reverse the delete. If you delete an item by mistake, immediately go to the Edit menu and choose Undo Delete.

Adjusting opening balances for balance sheet accounts

After creating your company in the Interview, you may need to enter additional opening balances or make adjustments to the account balances you've entered.

To adjust an opening balance for an account:
  i. From the Lists menu, choose Chart of Accounts
  ii. Double-click the account that should have an opening balance
  iii. Click anywhere in the blank entry at the end of the register
  iv. Change today's date to your QuickBooks start date
  v. Leave the Number and Payee fields blank
  vi. Enter the opening balance amount
      a. For bank accounts, enter the amount in the Deposit column
      b. For asset, liability or equity accounts, enter the amount in the Increase column
      c. For credit card accounts, enter the amount in the Charge column
  vii. In the Account field, choose Opening Bal Equity from the drop-down list

   Note that if you have not entered an opening balance for any of your accounts, you will have to create an Opening Bal Equity account
  viii. Click Record

Check the quantity of an inventory item

To check quantity on hand in the Item List:

    i.   Click Home

    ii.   In the Company section, click Items & Services

    iii.   Look in the On Hand column for the item

Adjust the quantity of an inventory item

To do this task

    i.   Go to the Vendors menu, then point to Inventory Activities, and then click Adjust Quantity/Value on Hand

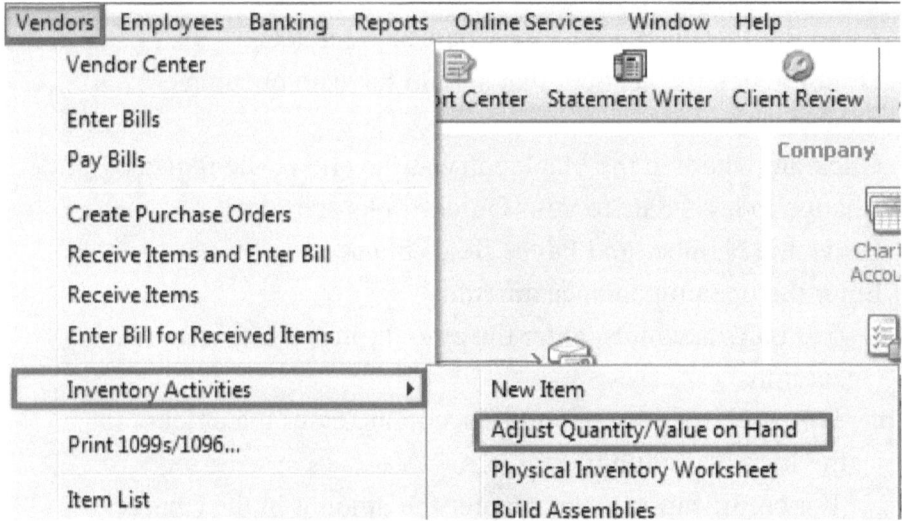

    ii.   Click the Adjustment Account drop-down arrow and then click the account where you want to track inventory adjustments

iii. If you use class tracking, click the Class drop-down arrow and then click a class

iv. In the New Qty column, enter the correct quantity

v. Enter a memo in the Memo field to remind yourself later why you made this quantity adjustment

vi. Save the adjustment

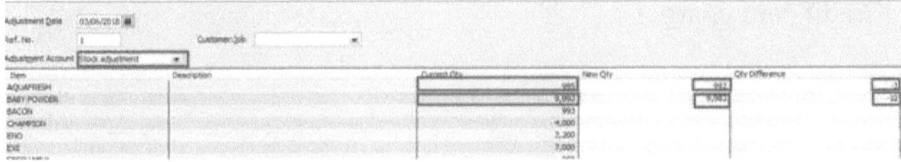

Purchase Forms

The purchase forms available in QuickBooks are:

i. Purchase orders

ii. Bills

iii. Credit card charges

iv. Checks

Purchase order

You use a purchase order to tell a vendor that you want to order goods or services.
Purchase orders help you keep track of what you have ordered and what you have already received. When you have received everything

on the purchase order, QuickBooks marks the purchase order as "Received in full."

When you receive the goods or services, QuickBooks uses information on the purchase order to enter a bill, check, or credit card charge for the same vendor.
When you use purchase orders to order inventory items, you can see not only how many items are in stock but how many are on order and when they're due to be received.
You can also use purchase orders to order services from a contractor, office supplies, a new asset for your company, or other items that are not set up as inventory in QuickBooks.

Turn purchase orders on and set preferences

To do this task:

    a.   Click on Edit and choose Preferences

    b.   Select the Items and Inventory

c. On Company preferences tab, check on Inventory and purchase orders are active checkbox

d. If you want to avoid entering duplicate purchase order numbers, select the Warn about duplicate purchase order numbers checkbox

e. Click OK

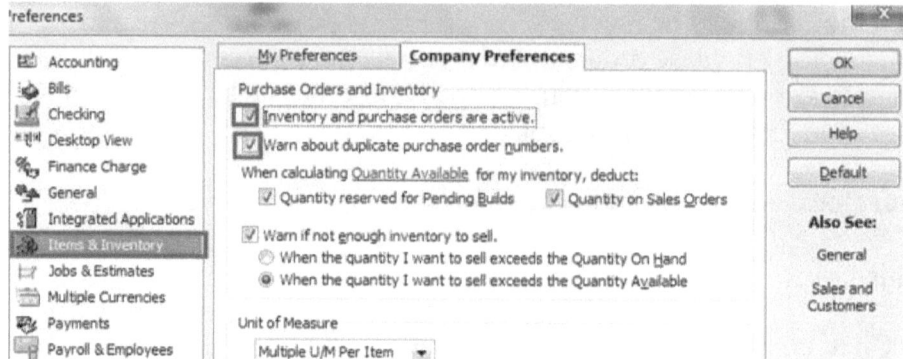

Create a purchase order

Go to the Vendors menu and click Create Purchase Orders.

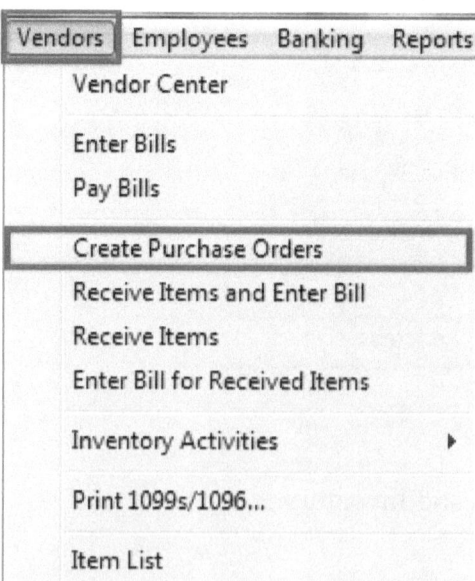

i. Click the Vendor drop-down arrow and choose an existing vendor or enter a new vendor.
ii. If you use class tracking, click the Class drop-down arrow and choose a class for this purchase order
iii. Confirm the purchase order date. QuickBooks puts the current system date
iv. Confirm the purchase order number. It uniquely identifies the purchase order
v. Describe the item that you want to order:
   a. Item- Lets you record the unique items.
   b. Description- Shows the description of item that you select.
   c. QTY- Lets you identify the quantity of the item that you want.
   d. Rate- Lets you enter the price per unit.
   e. Customer- Lets you identify the customer for whom the item is being purchased.
   f. Amount- Shows the total amount for the item. QuickBooks will multiply quantity by rate.

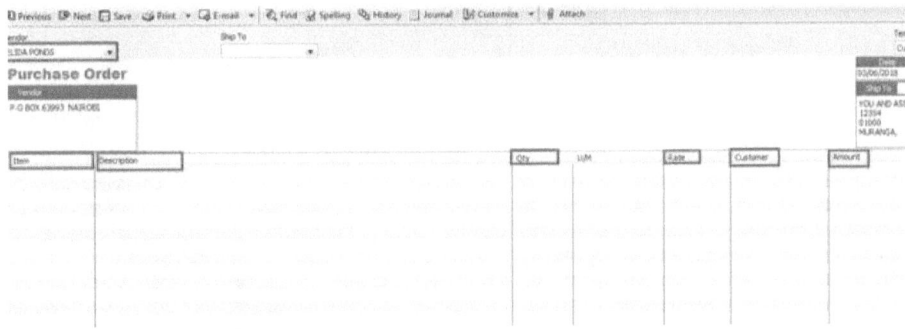

Order items for a specific job

To do this task:

i. Go to the Vendors menu and click Create Purchase Orders

    ii.   Fill out the purchase order form

    iii.   On the purchase order, specify the customer and job by doing one or both of the following:

          a. Specify that you want the vendor to ship the items directly to the customer by choosing the customer or job name in the Ship To field

          b. Enter a customer or job name in the Customer column

    iv.   Save the purchase order

Pay for items when you order them

To do this task:
    i.   Create a purchase order for the items

    ii.   Create another current asset account

        Name the account e.g. "Prepaid stock"
    iii. Enter charges for the items by:
          a. Writing a check

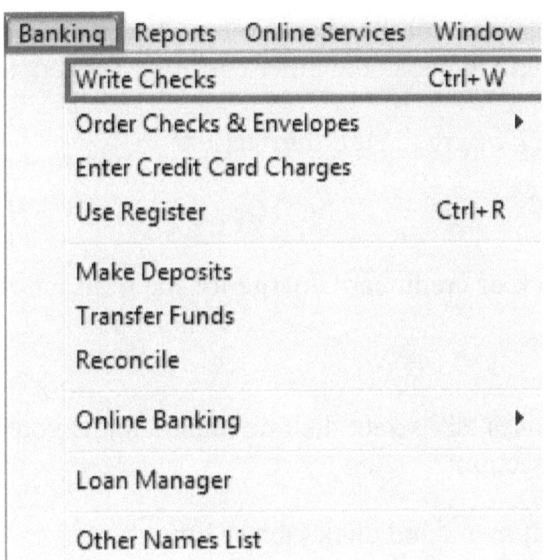

d. When QuickBooks indicates that you have an open purchase order for the vendor, do not select the purchase order

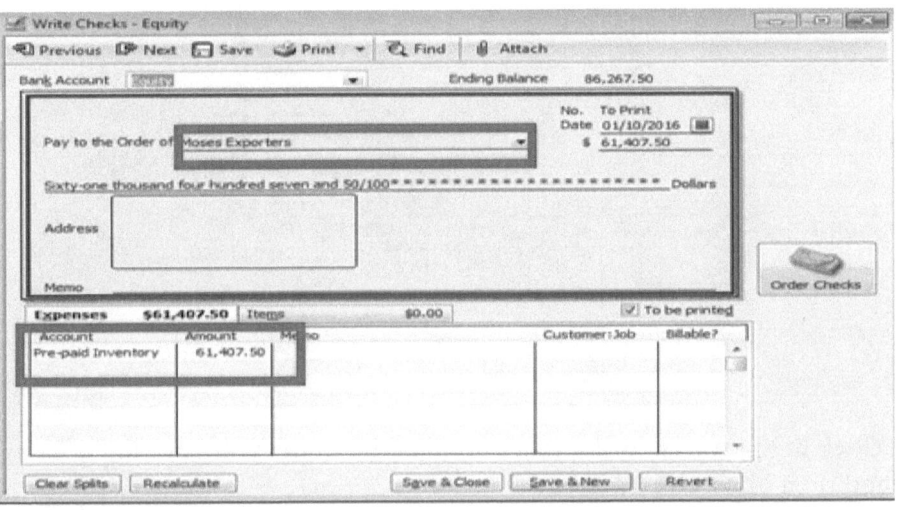

iv. On the Expenses tab of the check or credit card charge, click the Account field. Choose the other current asset account that you created

v. Save the check or credit card transaction

To receive the items

i. Find the check or credit card charge for the transaction

ii. On the Expenses tab, select the line that contains your other current asset account

iii. Go to the Edit menu and click Delete Line

iv. Click the Items tab

v. Click Select PO

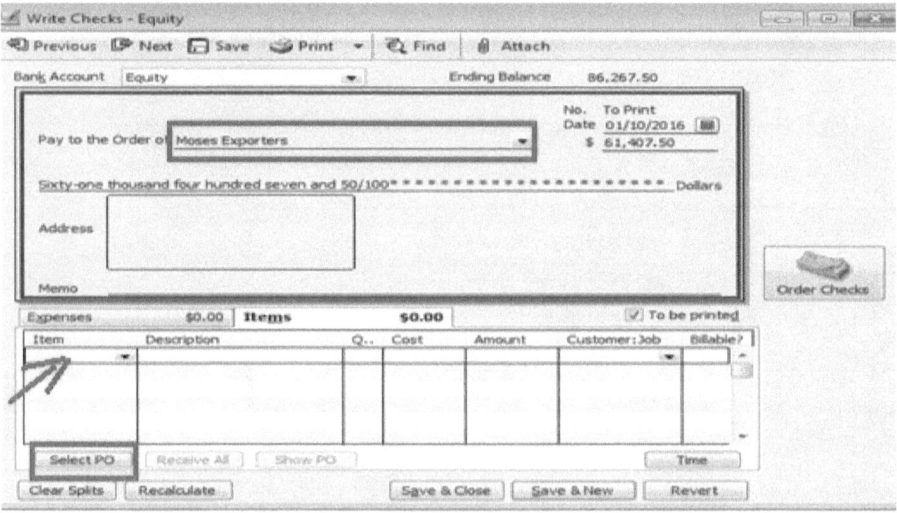

vi. Click the purchase order that contains the items you paid for and then click OK

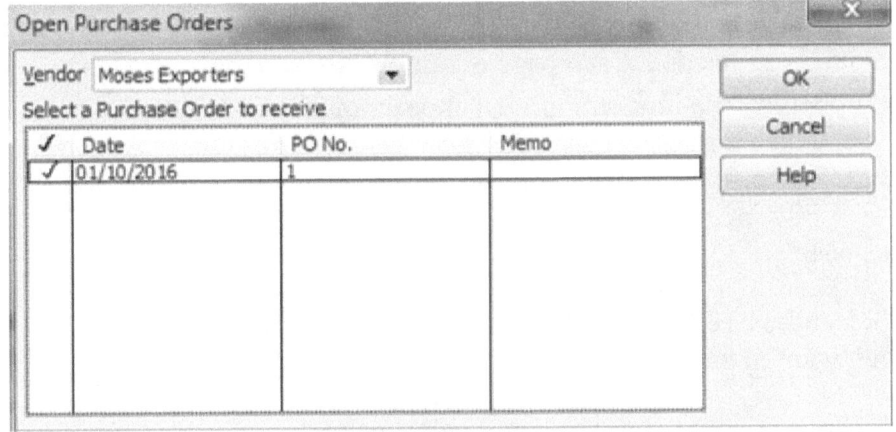

vii. If necessary, record additional expenses

> Don't add additional expenses to the existing credit card charge or check.

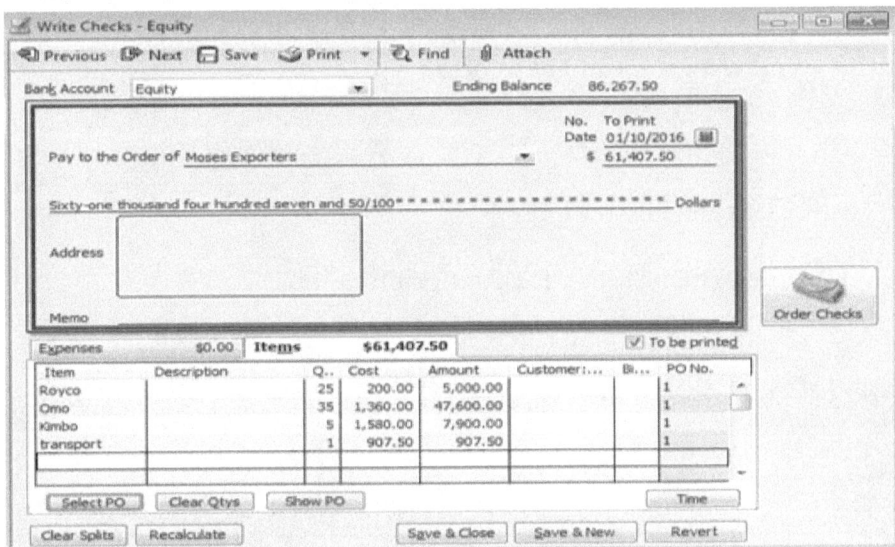

viii. Save the transaction

Multiple-page purchase orders

If a purchase order is too long to fit on one page, QuickBooks adds additional pages as needed. Each page of a multiple-page purchase order is numbered. The transaction total appears on the last page.

Print a batch of purchase orders

To do this task:

- a. Select the "To be printed" checkbox on each purchase order you want to print

- b. Make sure your printer has enough forms or paper to print the purchase orders

- c. Go to the File menu, click Print Forms, and then click Purchase Orders

- d. In the list that appears, make sure that all the purchase orders you want to print are selected

- e. Click the OK button

- f. Check the settings for your printing job

- g. Click the Print button

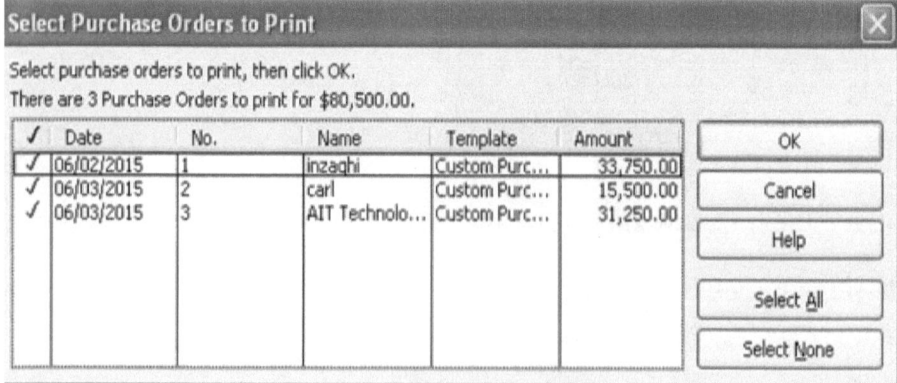

    i.   To print a particular purchase order, click to clear the checkmark next to the purchase order
    ii.   To print only a few purchase orders
    iii.   Click the Select None button
    iv.   Click each purchase order you want to print

Enter Bills and Pay bills

Before you can pay a bill, you need to enter it. You can enter a bill for items that you keep track of as part of your business or you can enter a bill for your expenses. Items are anything that your company buys, sells, or resells in the course of business, such as products. Expenses are all of the things you spend money on, and are linked to expense accounts. For example, if you pay for electricity.

Ways to pay bills

There are two ways to manage bill payments in QuickBooks:

    a.   Enter bills when you get them and pay them when they're due

          This method lets you keep your money in your business for as long as possible, and it enables you to track how much money you owe. You can run reports at any time to see how much you owe, and to whom. This method also keeps a record of all your bills, both before and after they're paid.

            i.   Use the Enter Bills window to enter bills into your Accounts Payable account

            ii.   Use the Pay Bills window to pay them when they're due

Note that, if you've entered a bill in the Enter Bills window, you should always use the Pay Bills window to pay that bill. Otherwise the bill will not be marked as paid.

b. Pay bills as soon as you receive them

   Use this method only if the bills have not been entered and you don't need to track them.

   i. If you're paying with cash, check, or any form of payment other than a credit card, use the Write Checks window

   ii. If you're paying the bill with a credit card, record the payment in the Enter Credit Card Charges window

In either window, assign the charge to an expense account.

Enter a bill for items

You can enter bills for your inventory and non-inventory parts, services, and fixed assets. Note that after you enter bills, they must be paid later using the Pay Bills window.

To do this task:

i. Go to the Vendors menu and click Enter Bills

ii. In the Vendor field, choose a vendor from the drop-down list, or choose <Add New> to enter a new vendor

iii. If you need to, you can change the date of the bill

   Entering the correct date will make it easier for you to track whether or not that bill has been paid, and if not, whether it is before or past the due date.

iv. In the Address field, enter or edit the vendor address if you need to

   Changes you make here will automatically update that vendor's record.

v. In the Amount Due field, enter the amount of the bill

vi. Complete the Ref. No, Terms, and Memo fields as necessary

vii. Click the Items tab. You can edit items that were entered from your purchase order, enter new items, or both

viii. To enter charges or taxes not associated with an individual item, click the Expenses tab. In the detail area, enter each charge, and associate it with its correct expense account

ix. Save the bill

When you save the bill, it appears in the unpaid bills detail report and the transaction list by vendor report. The expense of the items is reflected in your Profit and Loss report.

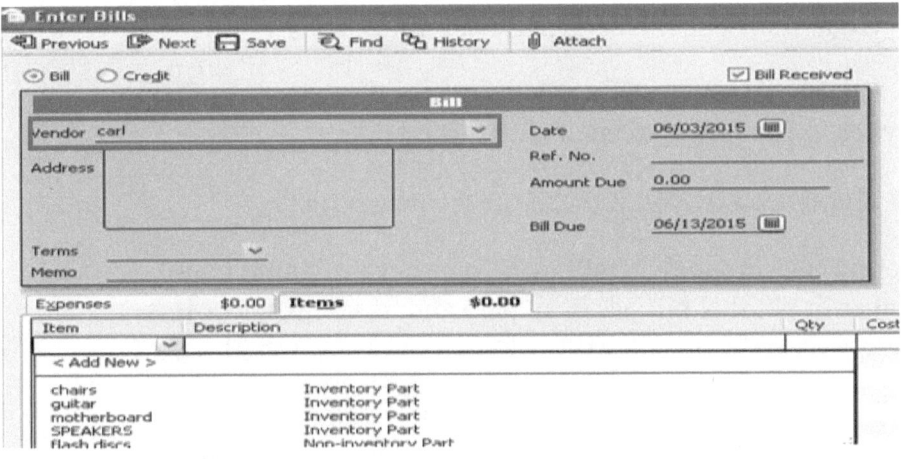

Receive against purchase orders

If an open purchase order exists for this vendor, you are prompted to receive against it.

To do this task:

i. Click Yes to receive against one or more purchase orders
ii. Click each purchase order that contains items you've received and are being billed for
iii. Click OK

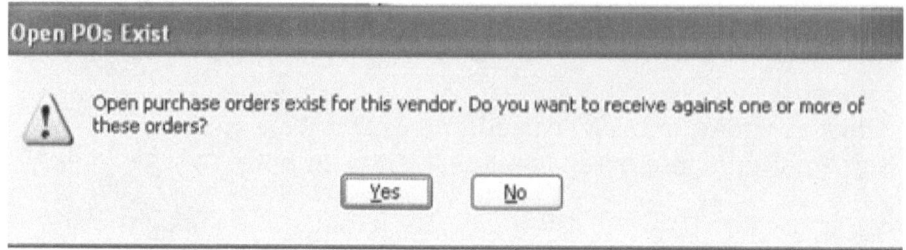

Enter a bill for expenses

Expenses are all of the things you spend money on, and are linked to one or more expense accounts. For example, if you pay electricity, assign that bill to an expense account set up for electricity.

To do this task:

i. Go to the Vendors menu and click Enter Bills

ii. Click the Vendor drop-down arrow and choose a vendor or click <Add New> to enter a new vendor

iii. If you need to, you can change the date of the bill

Entering the correct date will make it easier for you to track whether or not that bill has been paid and, if not, whether it is before or past the due date (how long it has been aging)

iv. In the Address field, enter or edit the vendor address if you need to. Any changes you make here will automatically update that vendor's record

v. In the Amount Due field, enter the amount of the bill

In the Expenses tab, click in the Account field and choose an expense account from the drop-down list.

vii.

viii. Save the bill

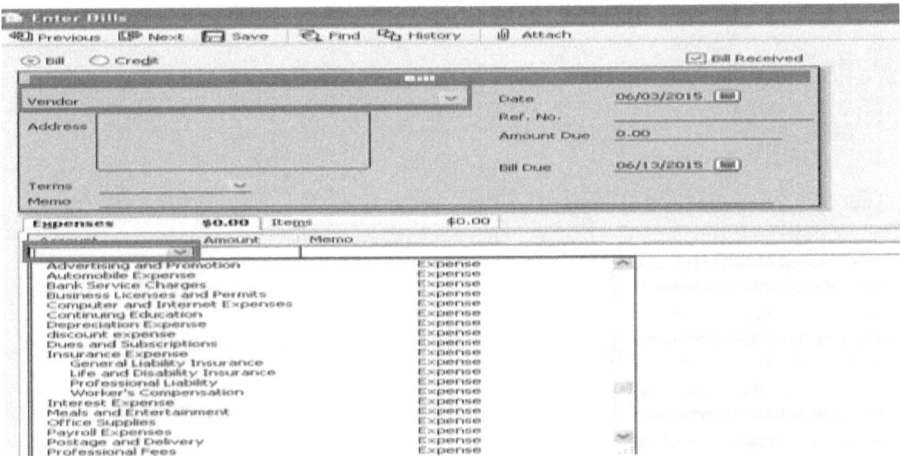

Void or delete a bill or payment

Voiding changes the amount of the bill or payment to zero, but keeps a record of it in QuickBooks.

Deleting permanently removes the bill or payment. When you delete a bill that you've already paid, QuickBooks creates a credit with the vendor. If you delete a payment, the bill (or bills) it was paying will show unpaid balances.

To do this task:

i. Open the Accounts Payable register

ii. Find the bill or payment in the register window

iii. Go to the Edit menu and click Void Bill or Void Bill Pmt to void the transaction, or click Delete Bill or Delete Bill Pmt. to delete the transaction

iv. Click Record to confirm your choice

Enter credit from a vendor

To do this task:

i. Go to the Vendors menu and click Enter Bills

ii. At the top of the Enter Bills window, click Credit

iii. Enter the vendor's name and the amount of the credit

iv. In the detail area, enter the expense accounts, customers, jobs, or classes to which you want to assign the credit

v. Save the credit

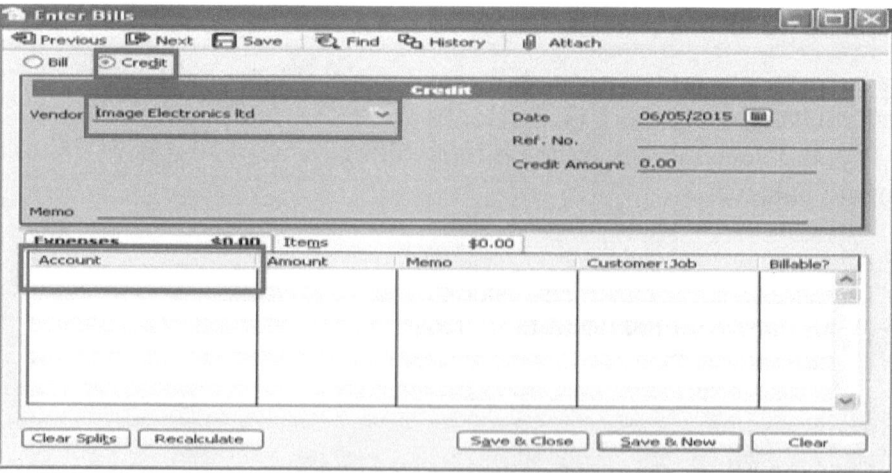

Apply credit from a vendor to a bill payment

To do this task:

i. Go to the Vendors menu and click Pay Bills

ii. Complete the bill payment information for payment by check, cash, credit card, but do not record the payment

iii. Select and highlight the bill to which you want to apply a credit

iv. Click the Set Credits button

v. In the Credits pane, select each credit that you want to use for this bill

vi. If you want to use only part of a credit, change its amount in the "Amt. To Use" column

vii. Click the Done button

viii. Finish paying the bill in the Pay Bills window

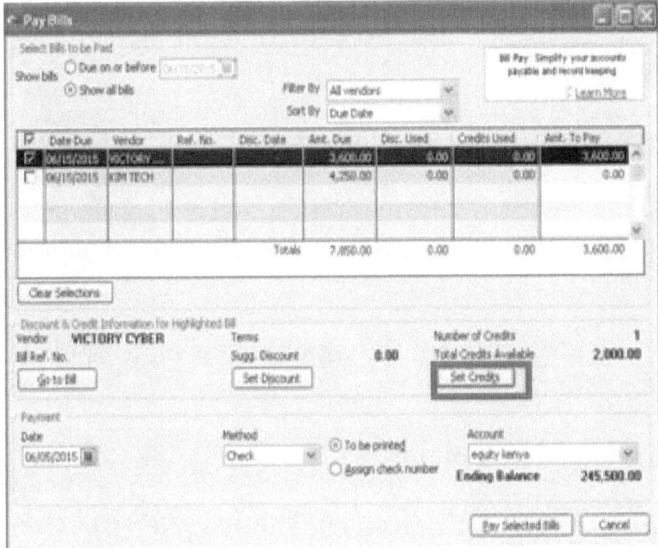

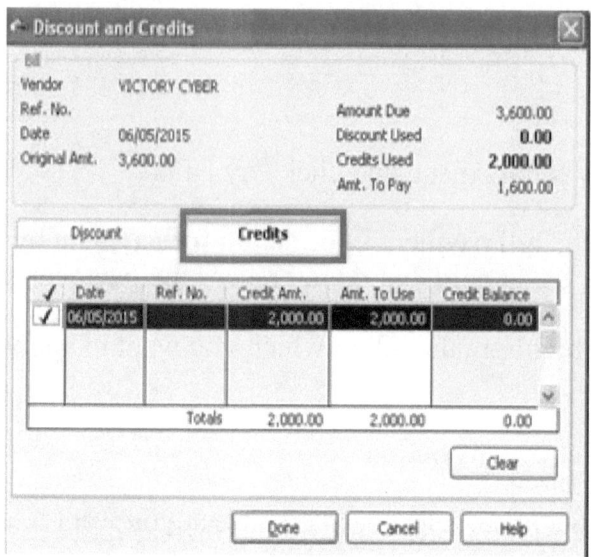

Apply a discount to a bill you pay

You can apply a discount from a vendor to one or more bills from that same vendor.

To do this task:

i. If you have not already done so, enter the bill in QuickBooks

ii. Go to the Vendors menu and click Pay Bills

iii. Complete the payment information for a check, cash, credit card, or online vendor payment, but don't record the payment yet

iv. Select and highlight the bill for which you want to apply a discount

v. Click the Set Discount button

vi. Change the amount of the discount(This is optional)

vii. Choose the Discount Account where you track income from discounts

viii. Click the Done button

ix. Click the Pay Selected Bills button

Changing the discount amount

QuickBooks calculates a suggested discount amount based on your payment terms with the vendor and with the payment date.

You can enter any discount amount you choose. The amount of the discount can't be more than the amount due.

Enter a bill against an item receipt

When you get a bill from a vendor for inventory items that you've already received into QuickBooks by creating an item receipt, you need to enter a bill in QuickBooks against that item receipt.

If you don't enter the bill against its corresponding item receipt, the same inventory items will be received twice into QuickBooks, making the transaction wrong.

To do this task:

i. Go to the Vendors menu and click Enter Bill for Received Items

ii. In the Select Item Receipt window, click the Vendor drop-down arrow and click the vendor

iii. Click the item receipt associated with the bill you received from the vendor and click OK to convert the item receipt into a bill

iv. Compare the information on the bill you received from the vendor to the information in the Enter Bills window and make any necessary changes

v. If the bill includes any non-item expenses, such as freight charges or sales tax, click the Expenses tab and enter each expense on a separate line i.e.

    a. Click the Account drop-down arrow and click the account you want the expense charged to

    b. Enter the amount

    c. When you finish entering expenses, click Recalculate to update the Amount Due

vi. Save the bill

Return items after you've entered a bill

When you return items from a vendor, you decrease your quantity on hand of the items you're returning and create a credit with the vendor.

To do this task:

i. Go to the Vendors menu and click Enter Bills

ii. Select Credit

iii. Enter the name of the vendor to whom you're returning items

iv. Click the Items tab

v. Enter the items you're returning

vi. Save the credit

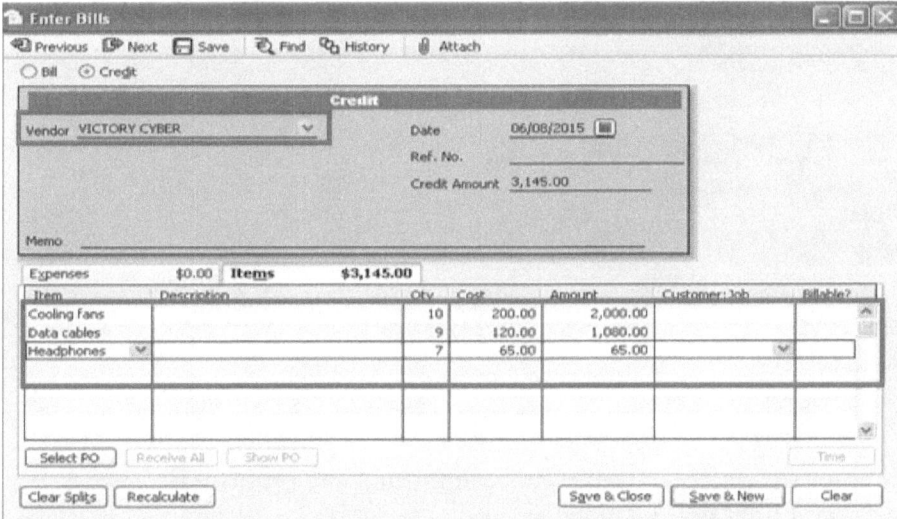

To apply credit from a vendor to a bill payment

i. Go to the Vendors menu and click Pay Bills

ii. Select and highlight the bill to which you want to apply a credit

iii. Click the Set Credits button

iv. In the Credits pane, select each credit that you want to use for this bill

v. Click the Done button

vi. Finish paying the bill in the Pay Bills window

View Unpaid Bills Report

i. Choose Vendors & Payables from the Reports menu
ii. Choose Unpaid Bills Detail

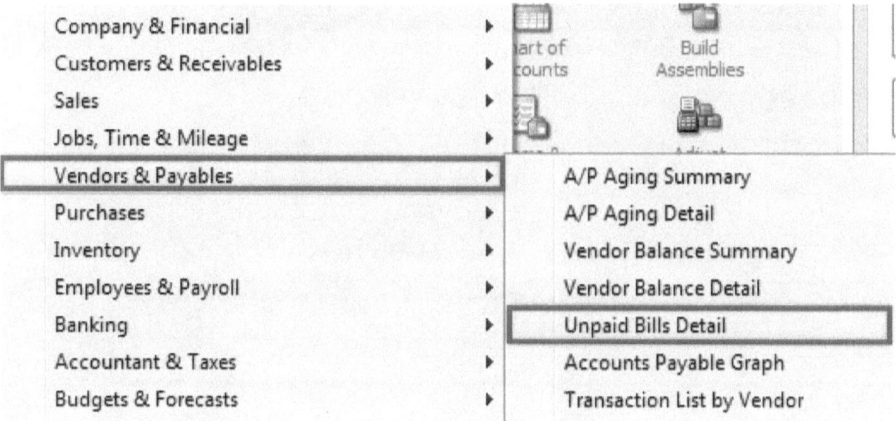

Select or enter the date. Click the Refreshbutton. The report will show all unpaid bills that have been entered as of that date.

Use the Pay Bills window to view and pay the bills you've entered in the Enter Bills window.
If you're sure you don't need to track your bills and bill payments, you can use the Write Checks or Enter Credit Card Charges window instead of using Enter Bills and then Pay Bills.

Sales Forms

The sales forms available in QuickBooks are:

a. **Sales receipts** used if you get paid immediately by cash, check, or credit card

b. **Invoices** used if you get paid later

c. **Credit memos** used for recording a return, a refund, or an overpayment

d. **Statements** or billing statements, for periodic billing or to let your customer know how much is past due

e. **Estimates** also known as bids, grants, or proposals, for describing work or products you propose to a customer

Invoices or sales receipts are the forms that you give to your customers to confirm their orders. Even if you do not want to give your customers a printed copy of the QuickBooks invoice, you should still use the invoice or sales receipt form to enter your sales into QuickBooks to keep your income information is up to date.

Invoices

If your customers don't pay you in full at the time you provide your service or product you need to track how much they owe you. Using an invoice helps you keep track of what your customers owe you, also known as accounts receivable.

To do this task:

i. Go to the Customers menu and click Create Invoices
The Create Invoices window opens. Click the Customer:Job drop-down list and select a customer or Select <Add New> to create a new customer or job.

ii. Enter the class information if you use class tracking

iii. In the detail area, enter the products and services for which you're invoicing

One can use a memo as a reminder and it is not shown on the printed invoice. It is displayed onscreen, on sales reports and, if you send reminder statements, it prints on reminder statements that include this invoice.
iii. Select the method you want to use to print and send the invoice to your customer

iv. Save the invoice

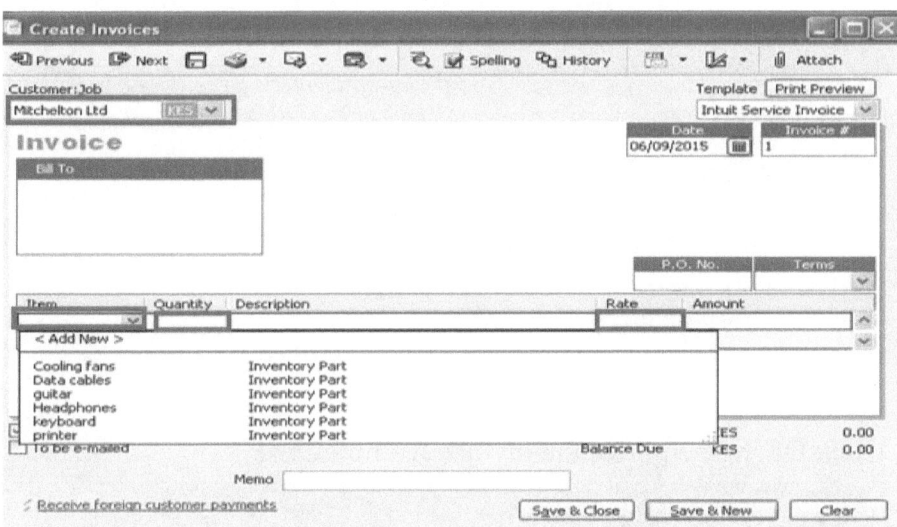

Create a recurring invoice

If you frequently enter the same line items on a transaction, you can memorize the transaction so that you won't have to re-enter it each time. If the amounts on the transaction do not change, you can fill in all the details for the transaction and can even have QuickBooks automatically enter the transaction for you.

If the amounts or other details sometimes change, you can enter the memorized transaction and leave some of the fields blank. When you want to use your memorized transaction, just choose it from your Memorized Transaction list. You can then edit it as needed.

To do this task:

i. Go to the Edit menu and click Memorize Invoice

ii. Enter a name that will help you recognize the invoice on the Memorized Transaction list

iii. Choose how you want QuickBooks to treat the invoice

   a. Remind me

   b. Don't remind me

   c. Automatically enter

iv. Click OK to memorize the invoice for future use

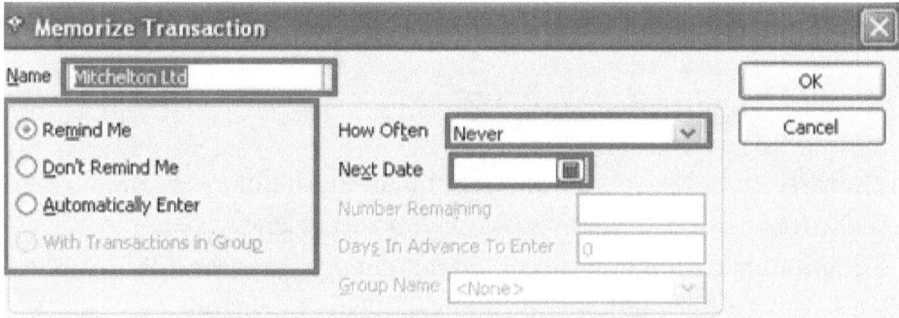

Entering a transaction from the Memorized Transaction list

This procedure assumes that you've already created the memorized transaction that you want to use.
   i. Go to the Lists menu and click Memorized Transaction List

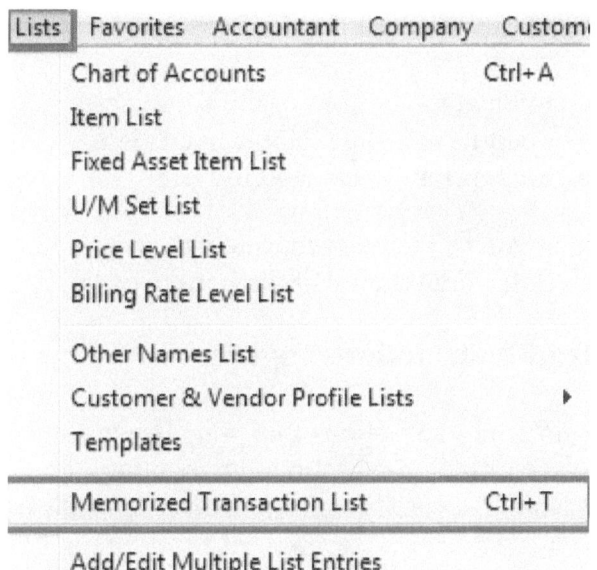

ii. Select the memorized transaction you want to use

iii. Click Enter Transaction

iv. Make any necessary changes or additions

v. Save the transaction

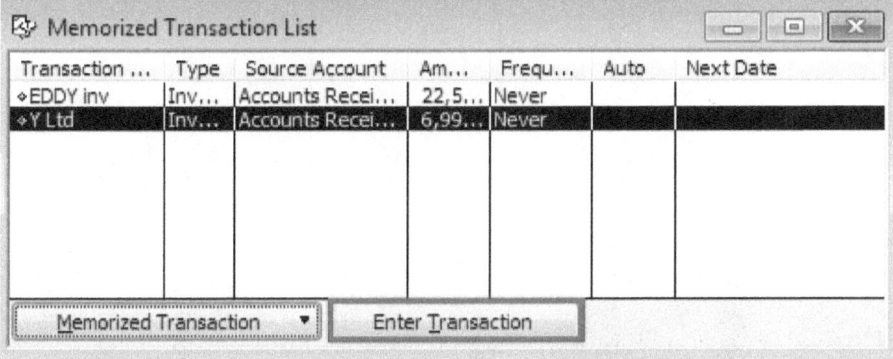

Manage your memorized transactions

Click Memorized Transaction at the bottom of the list to delete a memorized transaction or edit its schedule. You can create a memorized transaction group, print the list, and more.

To enter a transaction that you've memorized, select the transaction in the list and then click Enter Transaction at the bottom of the list.

Grouping memorized transactions together

If you have several memorized transactions that you always enter on the same day, you can save time if you group them together.

To do this task:

i. Go to the Lists menu and click Memorized Transaction List

ii. Click Memorized Transaction at the bottom of the list and click New Group

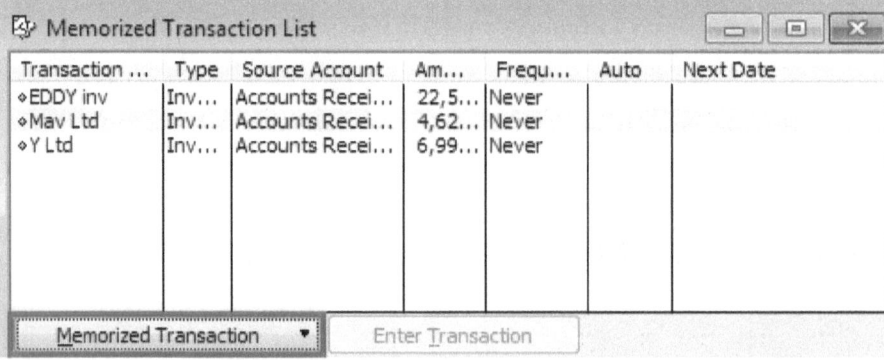

iii. Enter the name of the new group

iv. Choose how you want to manage the transaction group

You can have QuickBooks remind you about the transaction group on a regular basis, you can merely have the transaction group available for future use without being reminded about it or you can have QuickBooks record the transactions in the group on a regular basis.

v. Click OK

vi. Add, as needed, memorized transactions to the group:

    a. In the list, select the memorized transaction you want to add

    b. Click Memorized Transaction at the bottom of the list

    and click Edit

    c. Select "With transactions in group" and enter the name of the memorized transaction group

    d. Click OK

Rescheduling a memorized transaction

When you specify a schedule for a memorized transaction, you can choose whether QuickBooks should remind you of the transaction or automatically record it for you.

To do this task:

i. Go to the Lists menu and click Memorized Transaction List

ii. Select the memorized transaction whose schedule you want to change

iii. Click Memorized Transaction at the bottom of the list and click Edit

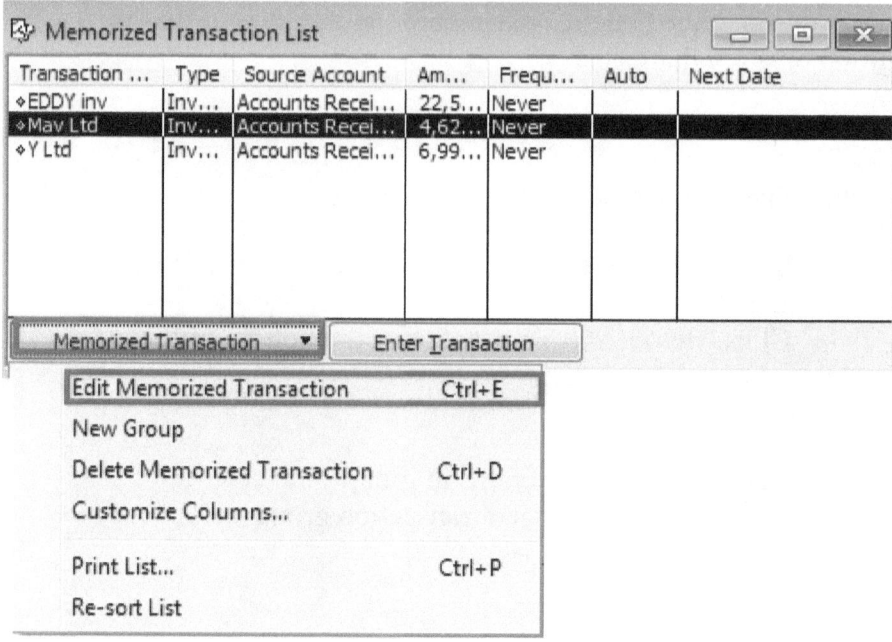

iv. Select a different scheduling option for the transaction

v. Click OK

How to change the content of a memorized transaction

To do this task:

i. Go to the Lists menu and click Memorized Transaction List

ii. Select the memorized invoice from the list

iii. Click Enter Transaction in the lower left corner of the list

iv. In the memorized invoice window, make the changes you want

v. Go to the Edit menu and click Memorize Invoice

vi. Indicate whether you want the new memorized invoice to replace the previous one

Print a memorized transaction list

To do this task:

i. Go to the Lists menu and click Memorized Transactions List

ii. Click Memorized Transaction at the bottom of the list and click Print List

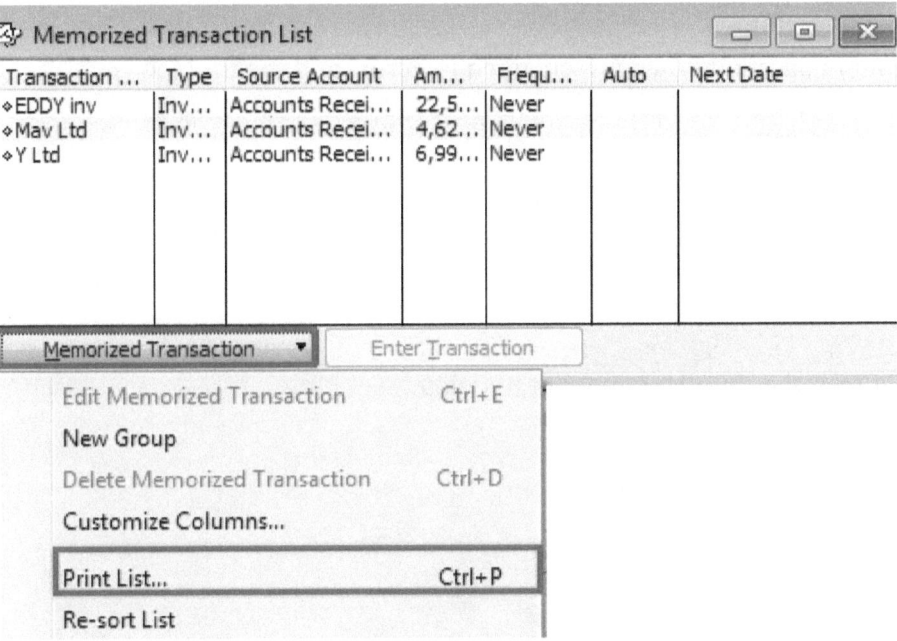

iii. In the Print List window, select the options you want and click Print

Void an invoice

To do this task:

i. Open the invoice you want to void

ii. Right-click in the Bill To (address) field and choose Void Invoice

iii. Save the change

The amounts on the invoice are changed to zeros, and the invoice is marked as "PAID".

Delete an invoice

Delete an invoice only if you haven't printed or saved it.

To do this task:

i. Open the invoice you want to delete

ii. Go to the Edit menu and click Delete Invoice

Record a partial payment using a payment item

A payment item subtracts the amount of a customer payment from the total amount of an invoice. If you receive full payment at the time of the sale, use a sales receipt form.

To do this task:

i. Create a payment item with a zero amount

ii. Enter the payment item on the invoice

iii. Enter the amount of the payment in the Rate column or Amount column, if there is no Rate column

QuickBooks automatically changes your entry to a negative number so the invoice will be correctly credited with the partial payment. The payment amount reduces the balance due on the invoice

iv. Print a copy of the invoice

v. Save the invoice

Receive payments

From the Customers menu, use the Receive Paymentsoption to record payments on account. When you use this feature to record payments, Cash is debited for the amount of the payment. The customer's receivable account is credited for the full amount of the invoice. If there is a sales discount, Sales Discount is debited for the discount amount.

To do this task:

i. From the Customersmenu, choose Receive Payments. The Receive Payments window will appear
ii. Complete the fields in the top half of the window. If the payment is for a particular job on your Customers & Jobs list, click the Received From drop-down list and choose the customer's name
iii. A check mark will appear to the left of the invoice. An underpayment warning will appear in the lower left corner of the Receive Paymentwindow

Underpayment KES 2,000.00. When you finish, do you want to:

◉ Leave this as an underpayment

◯ Write off the extra amount

[View Customer Contact Information]

iv. If you have not set your preferences to deposit to Undeposited Funds by default, you'll need to choose the bank account into which you want to deposit this payment
v. Save the payment

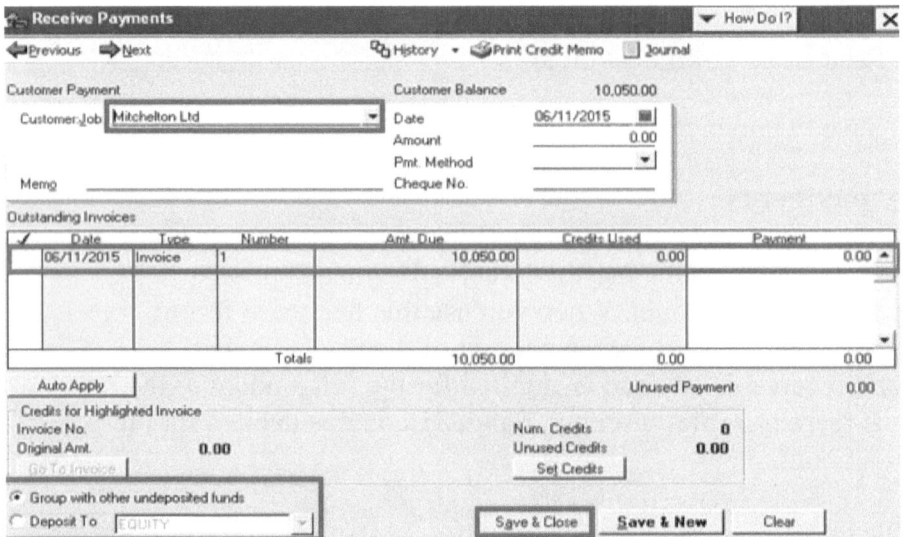

Discount and Credits
Apply a discount for early customer payment

Use Discount & Credits in the Receive Payments window to apply a discount for early payment for customers whose payment terms include a discount for payment before the due date.

Even if the customer has sent you a payment for the full amount of the invoice (or statement charges), you can apply a discount. QuickBooks holds any credit amount in accounts receivable until you apply it to an invoice or issue a refund check.

If you are offering a discount for something other than early payment, use a Discount item instead.

To do this task:

i. Go to the Customers menu and click Receive Payments

ii. Enter the customer's payment in the Receive Payments window

iii. Click the line of the invoice to which you want to apply the discount

iv. Click Discount & Credits

v. Change the amount of the discount

QuickBooks calculates a suggested discount amount based on your payment terms with the customer and the payment date. You can enter any discount amount you choose; you don't have to use the suggested amount. However, the amount of the discount cannot be higher than the original invoice.

vi. Enter the name of the expense account you use to track discounts, for example Discount Expense

vii. Click Done to record the discount

viii. Save the payment

Apply Credits

When a customer is paying an invoice for which partial credit was received, use the Discount & Creditsoption on the Receive Paymentswindow to process the transaction.

i. Go to the Customers menu and click Receive Payments

ii. In the Receive Payments window, click the Received From drop-down list and choose the customer to whom you're applying the credit

A note alerts you if the customer has available credit and the Customer balance field shows the amount available. If you don't specify the job, the Unused Credits field shows the total credits available for all jobs.

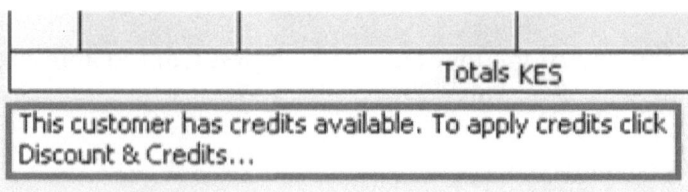

iii. Click in the Payment column to select the invoice or billing statement to which you want to apply the credit. Do not click in the checkmark column

iv. Click the Discount & Credits button

v. Click Done

vi. Save the credit

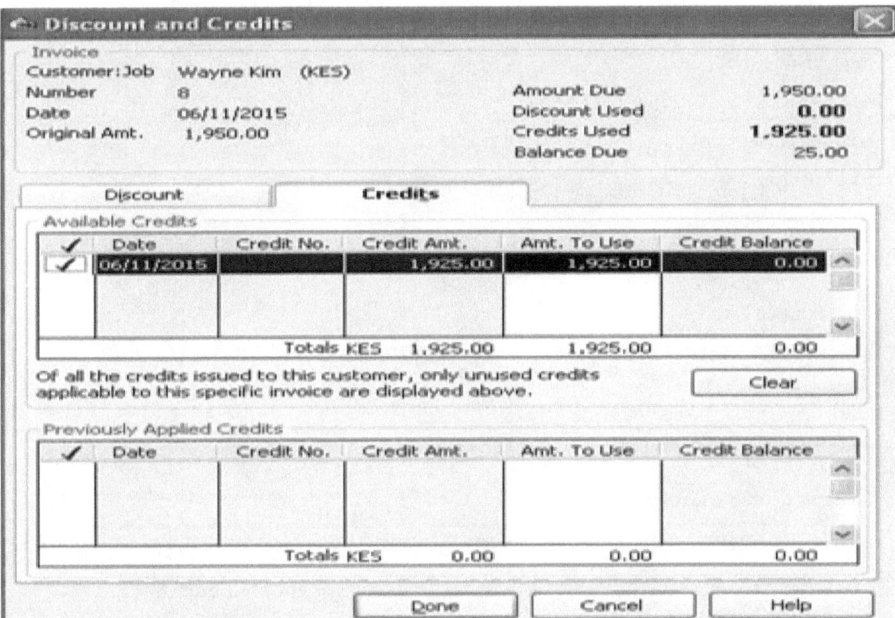

Set up payment terms

To do this task:
   i.   Go to the Lists menu, choose Customer & Vendor Profile Lists, and then click Terms List

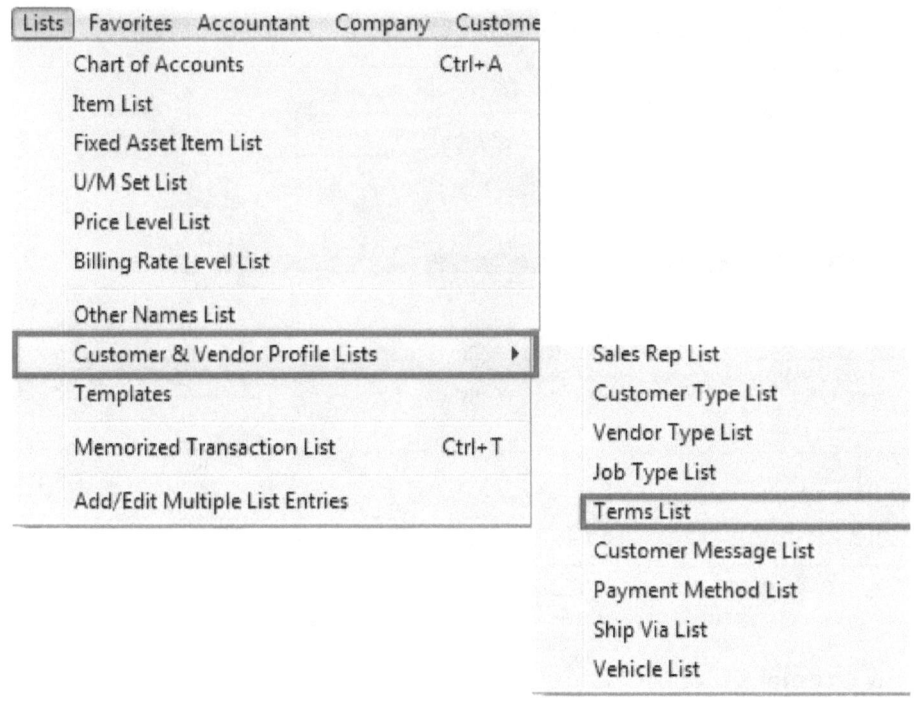

ii. Click Terms at the bottom of the list and click New

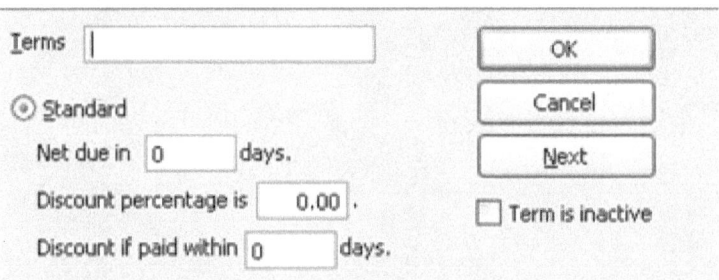

iii. In the Terms field, enter a word or phrase that will help you recognize the terms when you use the Terms list (what you enter here appears on the list)
iv. Indicate the type of terms that you want to use
  Standard vs. date-driven payment terms

v. Fill in the fields

vi. Record the payment terms

Associate terms with a vendor or a customer

To do this task:

i. Click Vendor Center to apply the terms for a vendor or Click Customer Center to apply to a customer

ii. Right-click the vendor or the customer that you want to associate with the terms and choose Edit Vendor or the customer

iii. Click the Additional Info tab and enter the terms you want to apply

Deposit customer payments

To do this task:

i. Go to the Banking menu and click Make Deposits

ii. If the Payments to Deposit window opens, select the payments from Undeposited Funds you want to deposit now, click OK, then continue with step 3. If the Payments to Deposit window do not open automatically, you don't currently have any payments in the Undeposited Funds account. Continue with step 3

To reopen the Payments to Deposit window at any time you have undeposited payments, click Payments in the Make Deposits window

iii. In the Make Deposits window, click the Deposit To list and choose the bank account you want to deposit into

iv. Enter the date and an optional memo

v. The Currency field matches the currency of the account selected in the Deposit To field and determines the currency of the deposit. Enter an exchange rate for foreign deposits. Home currency deposits always use an exchange rate of 1

vi. Add any additional payments to deposit

    a. Enter any deposits that did not come from customer payments

    b. Enter any cash amounts that you want to deposit. The cash amounts will be totaled and entered as one amount on the deposit slip

    c. If depositing a payment made by credit card, enter the credit card fees as a negative amount and change them to an expense account by listing the fees on a separate line here. You cannot deposit credit card payments when using a printable deposit slip

To return to the list of payments to deposit, click Payments on the window menu bar.

vii. If you are getting cash back from your deposit, fill in the cash back fields

viii. Print a record of the deposit

ix. Save the deposit

Enter Sales Receipts

If your customers pay in full at the time they receive your service or product, then you don't have to track how much they owe you. However, you might want to track each sale, calculate its sales tax, or print a receipt for the sale. In that case, use a sales receipt.

If customers pay in advance, either in part or in full, you should not use a sales receipt.
A cash sale, and using a sales receipt, requires full payment at the time you record the sale.
To do this task:
    i.   Go to the Customers menu and click Enter Sales Receipts

    ii.   Enter the name of the customer: job

    iii.   Select a class for the sale if necessary

    iv.   Fill in the top part of the sales form

v. In the detail area, enter the line items, that is, the products and services you're selling

vi.   Change any sales tax information if necessary

vii.   Select how you want to deposit the cash

viii.   Enter a memo for this sale

> The memo is a reminder to you. It is not shown on the printed form. It is displayed onscreen and on sales reports that include this sale.

ix.   Choose one of the following options:

        a.   Select the To be printed checkbox if you plan to print the sales receipt later

        b.   Print it now

xi. Save the transaction

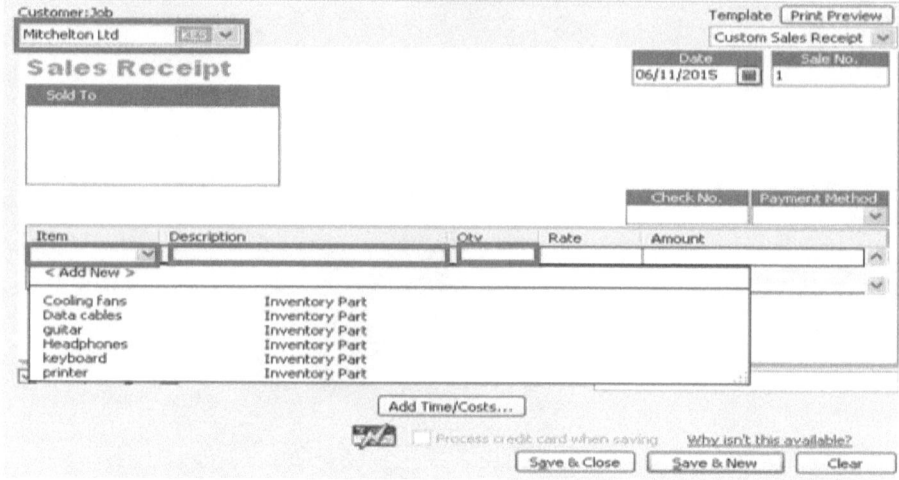

Note that when you save a sales receipt, QuickBooks does several things behind the scenes:

    a. QuickBooks tracks your sales and income from the sales receipt

    b. The sales by item summary report, which summarizes your sales subtotaled by the types of items you sell, increments the items that you sold

    c. The income accounts associated with the items sold increases, which you can see in your profit and loss report

If you have a transaction that you frequently enter, you can save time by memorizing it for future use. Deposit customer payments.

View funds in the Undeposited Funds register

QuickBooks lists any funds that you have grouped with other undeposited funds in the Undeposited Funds register. Use the register to see a list of all sales listed in the Undeposited Funds account. Any sales receipts that you chose to deposit directly to an account do not appear in this register.

To do this task:

i. Go to the Lists menu and click Chart of Accounts

ii. Select Undeposited Funds from the Accounts list

iii. Click Activities at the bottom of the list and click Use Register

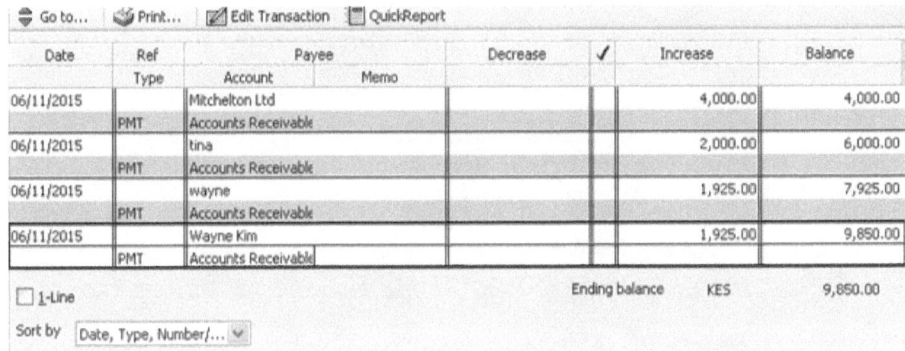

Credit memos

Enter a credit memo/refund to record a return when a customer returns items for which you have already recorded. You can also use a credit memo as part of the process of handling a bad or bounced check from a customer.

To do this task:
i. Go to the Customers menu and click Create Credit Memos/Refunds

ii. In the Customer:Job field, choose the customer and job for which you are creating the credit memo or refund check

iii. Enter the items being returned in the line item area

Use the same information that was on the original invoice or billing statement. QuickBooks decreases the income accounts of the invoice items by the amount of the return.

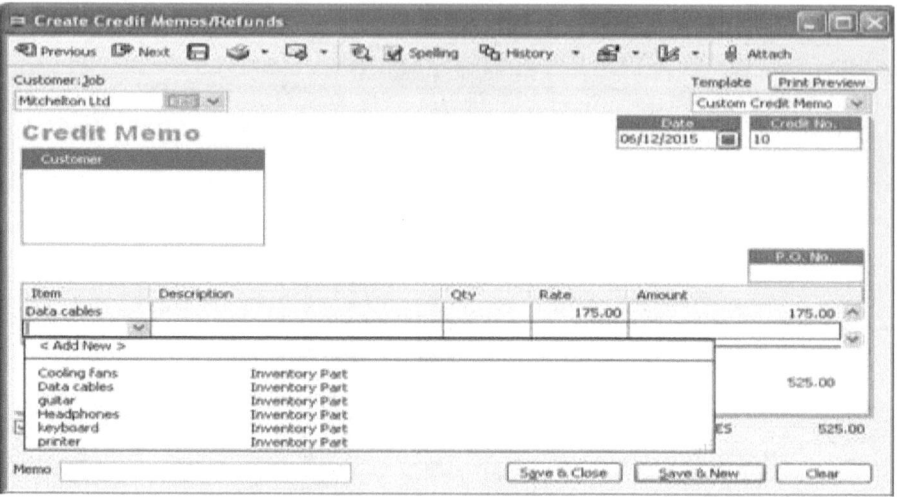

iv. In the Customer Message field click a message from the drop-down list, or enter a new message to your customer if necessary

v. Enter a memo for this transaction if necessary

The memo does not print on the credit memo, but it does appear in the Accounts Receivable register and in the customer register.

vi. Print the credit memo if necessary

vii. Save the credit memo

The Available Credit window opens, where you tell QuickBooks how to use this credit.

viii. Choose one of the following:

    a. Retain as an available credit

    b. Give a refund

    c. Apply to an invoice

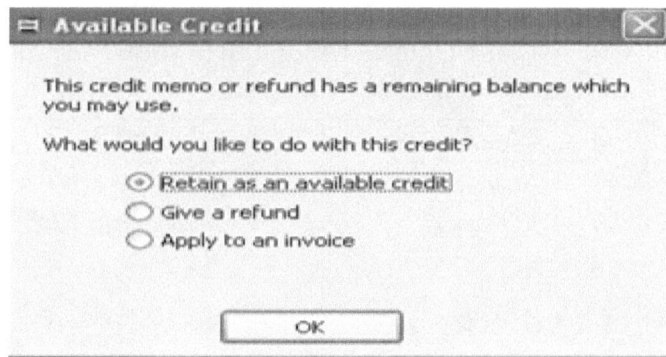

Handle returns on unpaid invoices

If your customer is returning items from an unpaid invoice, void the invoice. When you void the invoice instead of deleting it, you maintain complete records of all sales.

If the customer is returning items but there are items remaining on the invoice, do not void the invoice. Instead, create a credit memo/refund to record the returned items.

Use a customer credit as payment

If you previously created a credit memo for a customer, you can apply the amount of the credit memo to the unpaid invoices and billing statements for that customer.

To do this task:

i. Go to the Customers menu and click Receive Payments

ii. In the Receive Payments window, click the Received From drop-down list and choose the customer to whom you're applying the credit

   A note alerts you if the customer has available credit and the Customer balance field shows the amount available. If you don't specify the job, the Unused Credits field shows the total credits available for all jobs.

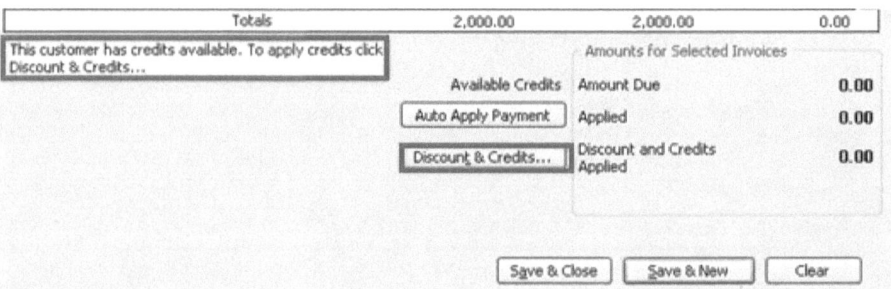

iii. Click in the Payment column to select the invoice or billing statement to which you want to apply the credit. Do not click in the checkmark column

iv. Click the Discount & Credits button

v. Click Done

vi. Save the credit

Edit a credit memo

To do this task:

i. Find the credit memo in the Customer Center or Accounts Receivable register

ii. Select the credit memo in the register

The credit memo transaction will be of type CREDMEM

iii. Go to the Edit menu and click Edit Credit Memo

Date	Number Type	Customer Description	Item	Qty	Rate	Amt Chrg Billed Date	Amt Paid Due Date
07/27/2015	2 INV	Erico				2,000.00	Paid
07/27/2015	1 CREDMEM	Erico				-3,500.00	07/27/2015
07/27/2015	Number	Customer Description	Item	Qty	Rate	Amt Chrg	

Statements

Use statements if you need to track how much your customers owe you (or accounts receivable, also called A/R), or if you receive payments in advance.

Use statements if you:

a. Need to track how much your customers owe you

b. Receive payments in advance

c. Accumulate charges before requesting payment

d. Need to show customers a history of their account activity that is charges, payments, and balance

To do this task:

i. Go to the Customers menu and click Create Statements

ii. If QuickBooks displays a choice of accounts, choose the A/R account for the statements that you want to print

QuickBooks displays the A/R Account field only when your chart of accounts contains more than one accounts receivable account.

    iii.   Verify that the statement date is the one that you want to use

Note that the statement date field is displayed on the top of the printed statements and in the Billed Date field of each customer's register. If you change the date, you are also changing the date due for statement charges.

    iv.   Choose to create statements for transactions within a specified date period

    v.   Create statements for all open transactions as of the statement date if necessary

    vi.   Choose the customers for whom you want to print statements

    vii.   Click the Template drop-down list and choose the template that you want to use to print the statements

    viii.   If you don't want QuickBooks to print statements for customers with a zero balance, select the option to exclude them

    ix.   Choose from the following additional options:

        a.   Show invoice details on statements

        b.   Print statements by zip code

    c.   Exclude customers with a balance less than a specific amount, no account activity, or customers marked inactive

x.   Click Assess Finance Charges to add finance charges to the statements if necessary

xi.   Click Preview to review the information that will appear on the statements

xii.   Click Print or E-mail, depending on how you want to send the statements to your customers

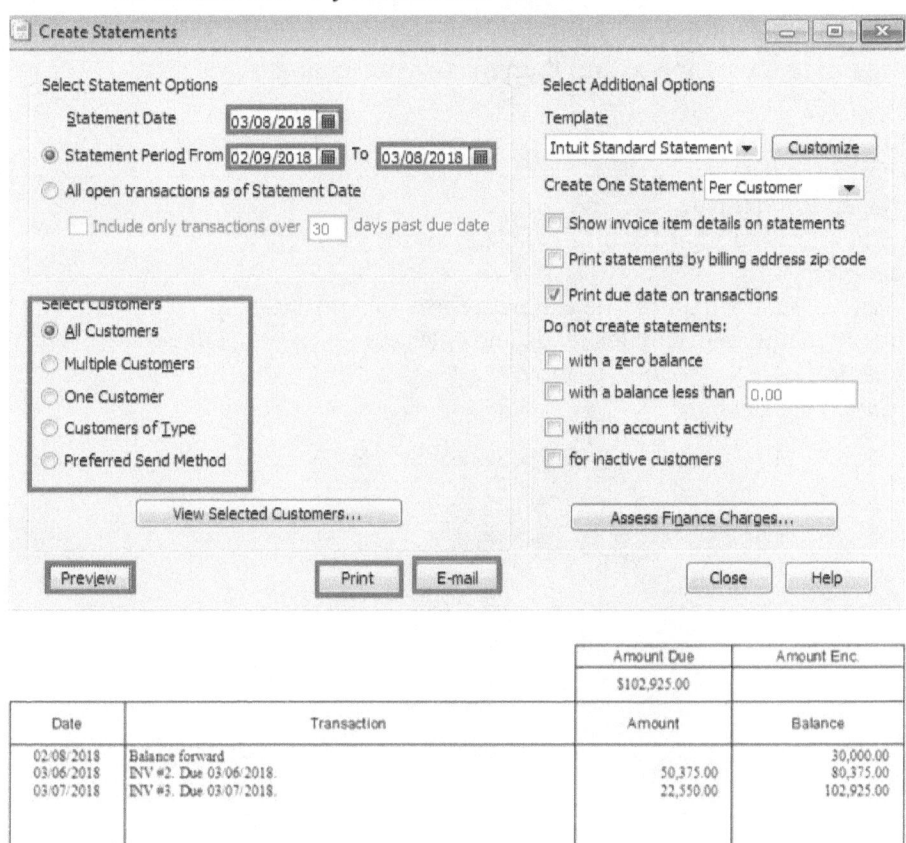

91

Estimate

Create an estimate when you want to give your customer a quote, bid, or proposal for work you plan to do. The estimate form looks very much like an invoice; however, its purpose is to help you begin negotiations with your customer.

After you've done the work or performed the service and you're ready to bill your customer, you can add data from the estimate to an invoice, eliminating the need to re-enter the information.

QuickBooks allows only one estimate per job, when you change an estimate; the revised estimate replaces the original.

If you want to create another version of the estimate instead, you should duplicate the estimate and then make your changes.

To do this task:

   i. Open the estimate
   ii. Click Print to print the original estimate for your records if necessary
   iii. Enter your changes on the estimate form. QuickBooks automatically recalculates totals and sales tax when you make changes
   iv. Save your changes

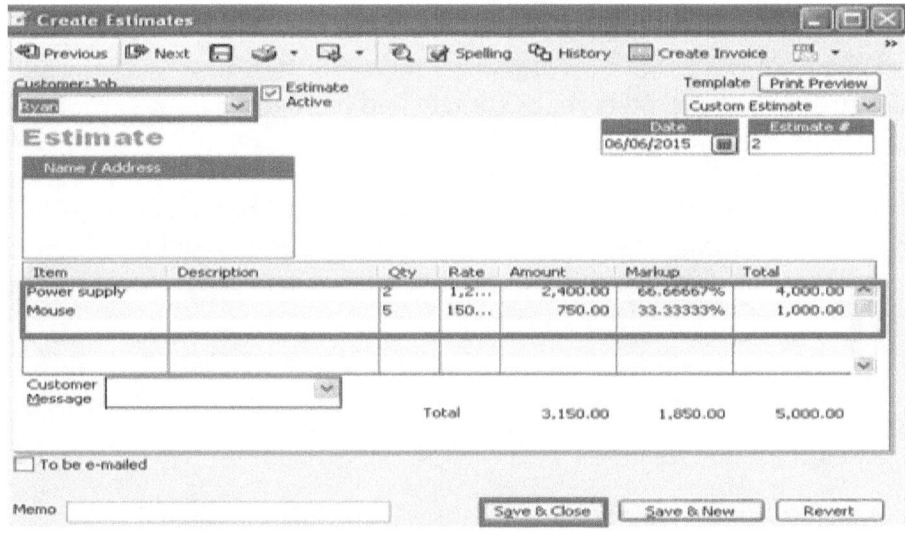

Make sure the estimates feature is turned on.

Turn on the feature:

i. Go to the Edit menu and click Preferences

ii. In the Preferences window, click Jobs & Estimates in the list on the left

iii. Click the Company Preferences tab

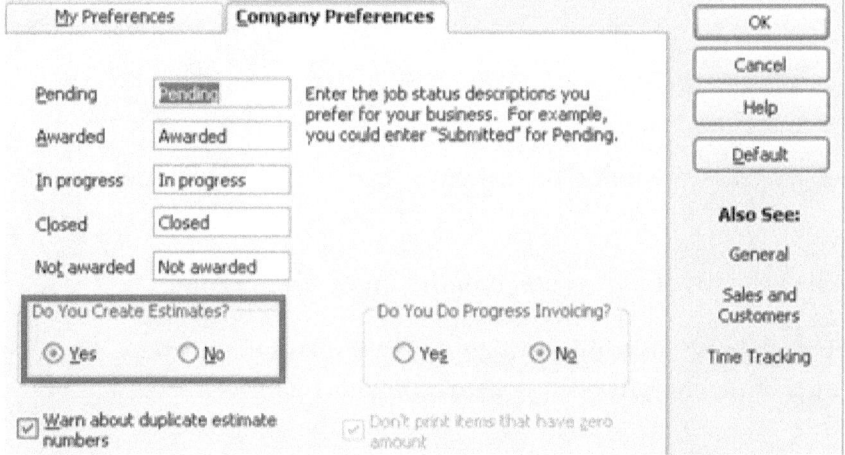

Create an invoice from an estimate

When a customer has accepted your estimate and has agreed to pay, you can turn the entire estimate into an invoice.

Progress invoicing, also called progress billing or partial billing, is invoicing from an estimate in stages instead of for the full amount. However, you can invoice for the full amount when using progress invoicing.

To do this task:

    i.   Open the estimate

    ii.   Click Create Invoice at the top of the estimate form

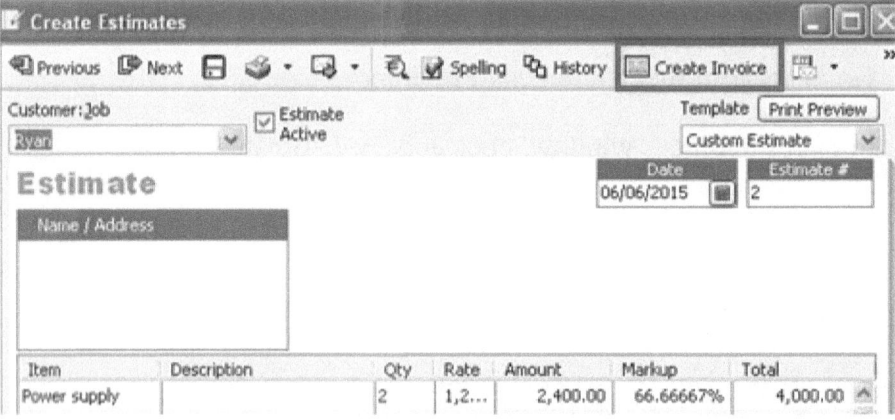

If you have progress invoicing turned on, specify what to include on the invoice.

    iii.   When the invoice appears, edit the invoice as needed

    iv.   Click Print to print the invoice now, or select the To be printed checkbox to print it with a batch of invoices later

    v.   Save the invoice

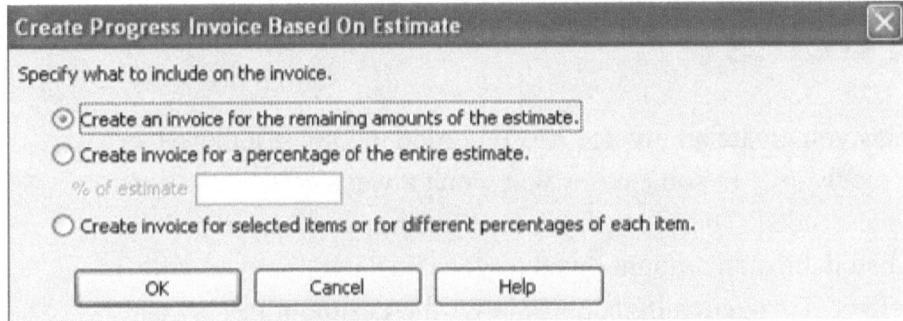

Delete an estimate

Deleting an estimate removes it completely from QuickBooks. Do not delete estimates that you may want to turn into invoices or see in reports. Delete only estimates that you no longer need for invoicing or reporting purposes.

To do this task:

i. Click Customer Center

ii. Select the customer or job whose estimate you want to delete

iii. Click the Show drop-down arrow and then click Estimates

iv. Double-click the estimate you want to delete

v. Go to the Edit menu and click Delete Estimate

vi. Close the Create Estimates window

Bad debts

As soon as you create an invoice it is recorded in QuickBooks as an account receivable. In some cases you won't always collect all credit you have extended. Therefore, from time to time you'll have bad debt. A bad debt is an amount owed to your business that you will never collect. This generally happens after the customer has been declared bankrupt or the cost to hunt them down and attempt to collect the balance exceeds the debt itself. You write off the loss to the business as an expense. It's done by crediting the customer's account therefore eliminating any balance remaining in that account.

To do this task:

i. First create an Other charge item that points to the expense account you want to use to track bad debts

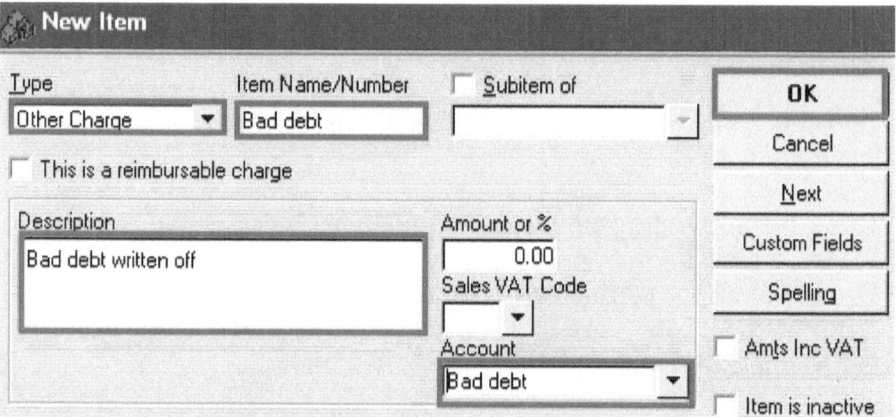

ii. Open credit Memo
iii. Choose the appropriate customer from customer job
iv. Choose the bad debt item you created in (i) above
v. Enter the amount to be written off in the amount column
vi. Click save and close

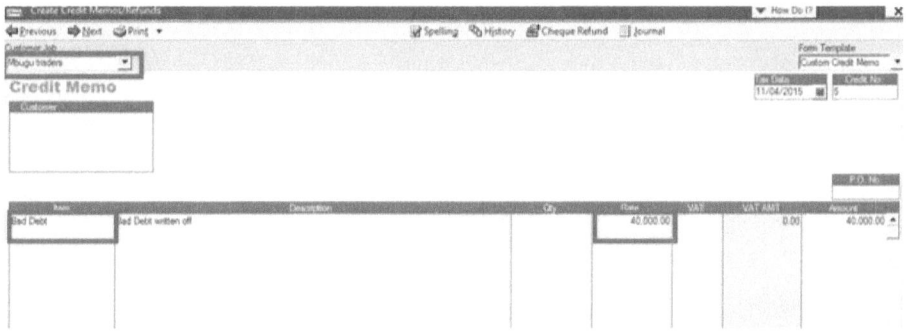

This will write off the amount that you will never collect. The customer's balance will reduce by the amount written off and profit and loss report will display the amount as an expense.

To Record a Bounced Cheque

Non-Sufficient Funds (NSF). This is a term used banking industry meaning a demand for a payment cannot be honored due to insufficient funds in the account on which the cheque was drawn or the amount written on the cheque exceeds the available balance. Also referred to as bad cheque, dishonored cheque. The cheque writer may be charged a fee by the financial institution. The customer may not have been aware of the insufficient funds.

When a customer's check is returned for insufficient funds, perform the steps described in this procedure.

To do this task:

        i.   Create an Other Charge item and give it a descriptive name e.g. "Bounced Check." For tracking bounced cheque.

a. In the Amount field, leave a zero amount

b. In the Account field, choose your bank account

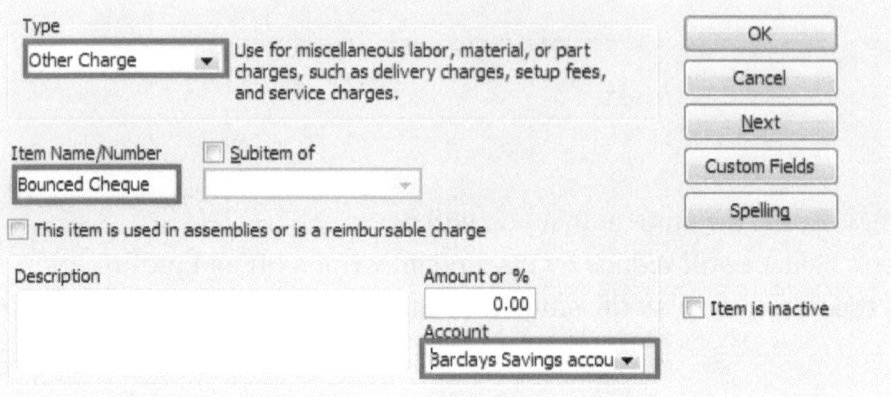

ii. Click Next

iii. Create a second Other Charge item titled "Bad Check Charge" for the service charge you assess customers for bounced checks. Link the new account item to an income account such as Retuned check charges. Use the item when you reinvoice the customer to recover the service charge

a. In the Amount field, leave a zero amount

b. From the Tax Code list, choose Non

c. In the Account field, choose an income account, such as Returned Check Charges. If the account doesn't exist, set it up

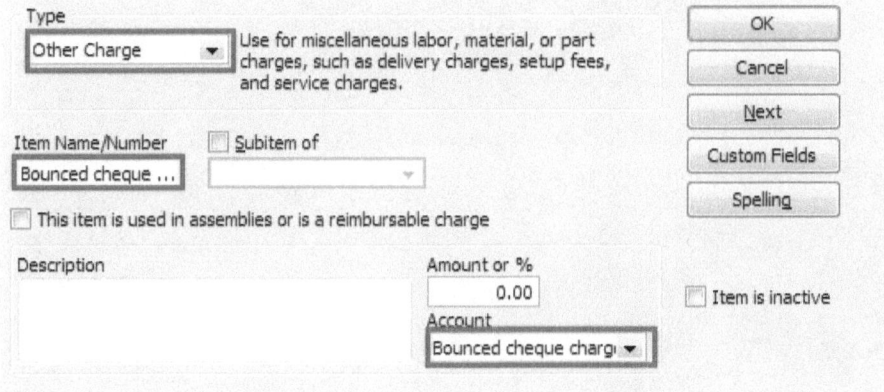

iv. Click OK

v. Re-invoice the customer :

　　a. Select "Create invoice"

　　b. Select the customer name

　　c. On the item drop down box, select the bad check item you created. This will reduce the bank balance by the amount of the returned cheque

vi. In the second line select the "Bounced cheque charge" item to charge the customer for returned cheque fees. Click "Print" from "Create invoice" main menu to print or "Save and Close" to Exit

This will include an income in the profit and loss report.

YOU AND ASSOCIATION WHOLESALES
Profit & Loss Detail
January 1 through March 7, 2018

Type	Date	Num	Adj	Name	Memo	Clr	Split	Debit	Credit	Balance
Ordinary Income/Expense										
Income										
Bounced cheque charges										
Invoice	03/07/2018	6		Mavuno Ltd			Accounts Re...		115.50	115.50
Total Bounced cheque charges								0.00	115.50	115.50

Fixed Assets

A fixed asset is a property used in a productive capacity that will benefit your business for longer than one year. They include such things as vehicles, furniture, equipment and so forth.

It is important to correctly record a new fixed asset in order to ensure an accurate balance sheet.

A journal entry is the easiest method because it allows you to create both the asset and corresponding loan balance. It is the best method to use if financing is involved with the asset's purchase.

You can also record information about your asset as you pay for it from any one of the following QuickBooks forms:

   a. Items tab of the Enter Bills window

   b. Items tab of the Write Checks window

   c. Items tab of the Enter Credit Charges window

   d. Item column of the purchase window

Note that transactions using fixed assets do not support QTY or Quantity.

To record a purchase of a fixed asset

Using a journal entry

Typically, you must depreciate fixed assets, and you also need to record the disposal of the fixed assets at some point in future for either a gain or a loss.

If you purchase a delivery truck for 1,200,000 for example, the journal entry that you use to record this purchase debits delivery truck for 1,200,000 and credits bank account for 1,200,000.

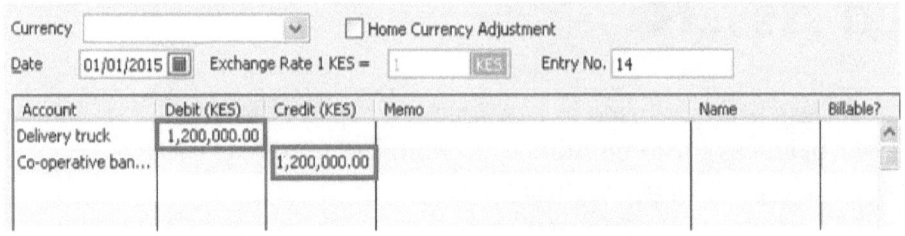

If you buy a delivery truck, you set up a fixed account for that specific delivery truck. i.e. any fixed asset that you buy individually or dispose of later individually needs its own asset account.

Set up asset accounts to track depreciation

    i. Create a fixed asset account for each asset (or group of assets) that you want to depreciate. For example, you might create a fixed asset account called Vehicles, or Computers

    ii. Add two subaccounts to each asset account that you created. One subaccount tracks the cost of the asset, the other tracks accumulated depreciation

    iii. Finally, create an expense account to track depreciation expense. Give the account a name such as Depreciation Expense

To record a Fixed asset using QuickBooks Forms

        a. On the item column click "Add New"

        b. Select Fixed Asset as the item type

c. In the name/number field enter an identifying name or number for your fixed asset. This appears on the fixed asset item reports

d. Click the Asset Account drop-down list and choose an asset account or create a new one

e. Enter purchase information and asset information

f. Leave the sales information blank and click Ok

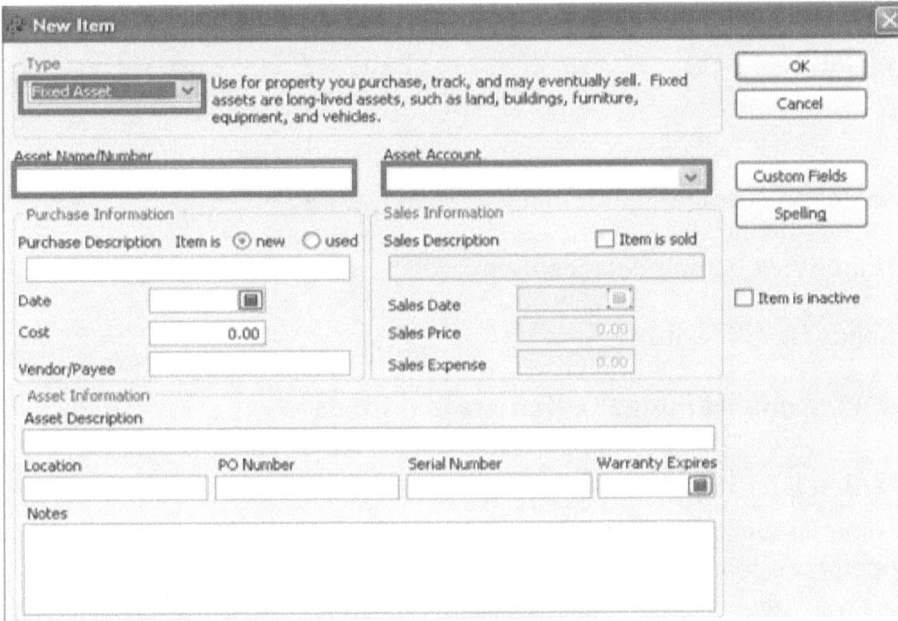

Buy fixed assets for your business

If you personally own assets that you want to transfer to your business or if you purchase a fixed asset for your business with personal funds, you'll need to set up fixed asset accounts. If you plan to track depreciation, set up separate subaccounts for original costs and for accumulated depreciation.

Add an entry to your Company Owes Me account. To create this account:

i. Go to the Lists menu and click Chart of Accounts

ii. Click Account at the bottom of the list and click New

iii. Select Other account types, and then click Other Current Liability.

iv. Click Continue

v. Enter an account name such as Amount Owed

vi. Enter the opening balance if any

vii. Click Save & Close

To enter a fixed asset bought with personal funds

i. Go to the Lists menu and click Chart of Accounts

ii. Double-click the account you created for owed amount to open the account's register

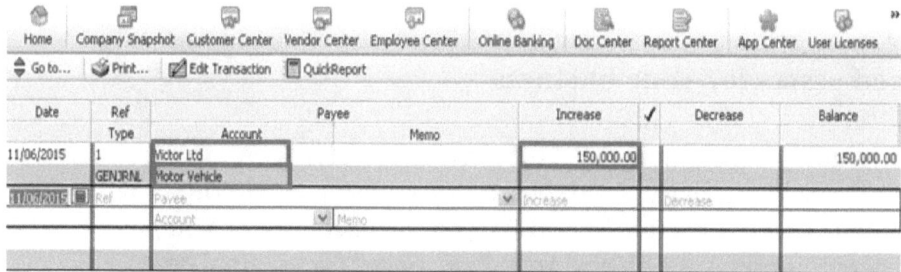

iii. Enter the name of the payee if necessary

iv. In the Increase column, enter the price you paid, and tab to the next line

v. Click the Account drop-down list and choose the appropriate Asset account

vi. Enter a memo if necessary

vii. Click Record

You will need to create a fixed asset item to track associated costs, depreciation, and so on, for your asset.

For personal assets that you want to transfer to your business

After you have entered the entire asset account information into QuickBooks, add an entry to an equity account. The transfer of a personal asset is an investment in your business, so you use an equity account, instead of the Company Owes Me liability account.

To transfer a fixed asset from your personal holdings to your business

i. Go to the Lists menu and click Chart of Accounts

ii. Double-click the equity account that you use to track owner investments, to open the account's register

iii. Enter your name if necessary

iv. In the Increase column, enter the depreciated amount of the asset, and tab to the next line

v. Click the Account drop-down list and choose the appropriate asset account

vi. Enter a memo if necessary

Date	Number	Payee		Increase	✓	Decrease	Balance
	Type	Account	Memo				
11/05/2015				250,000.00			250,000.00
	DEP	Co-operative bank:Savings Accouu Account Opening Balance					
11/05/2015				180,000.00			430,000.00
	DEP	Co-operative bank:Current Accoun Account Opening Balance					
11/06/2015	2	Peter		300,000.00			730,000.00
	GENJRNL	Motor Vehicle					
11/06/2015	Number	Payee		Increase		Decrease	
		Account	Memo				

    vii.   Click Record

You will need to create a fixed asset item to track associated costs, depreciation, and so on, for your asset.

Record thefts or losses of fixed assets

To do this task:

i. Go to the Company menu and click Make General Journal Entries

ii. In the Make General Journal Entries window, click in the Account column

iii. Click the Account drop down arrow and choose the fixed asset account or subaccount where you track the cost of the asset

iv. In the Credit column, enter the cost or starting value if you track depreciation in a separate asset account. Otherwise, enter the current book value of the asset

v. In the Name column, enter the name of the asset if necessary

vi. If you track accumulated depreciation in a separate subaccount, fill in a second line

vii. In the Account column, choose the Other Expense account for thefts or losses

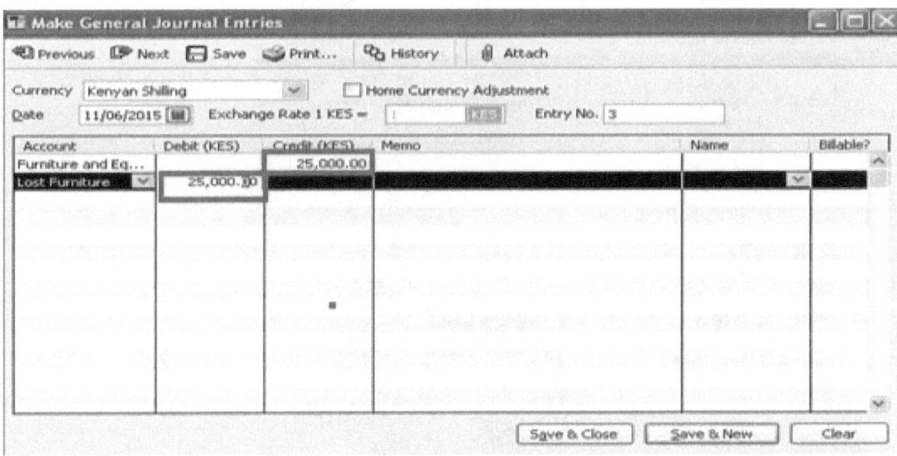

viii. Save the entry

Sell an asset

The process that you use to sell a fixed asset depends on how you track the asset's cost and depreciation. For example, if you track fixed assets by using fixed asset items, you must record the sale of the fixed asset item; while if you use a fixed asset account only to track your fixed assets, you can jump directly to recording the sale with a general journal entry.

Record the sale using the fixed asset item

If you use items to track your fixed assets, first follow these steps:

i. Go to the Lists menu and click Fixed Asset Item List

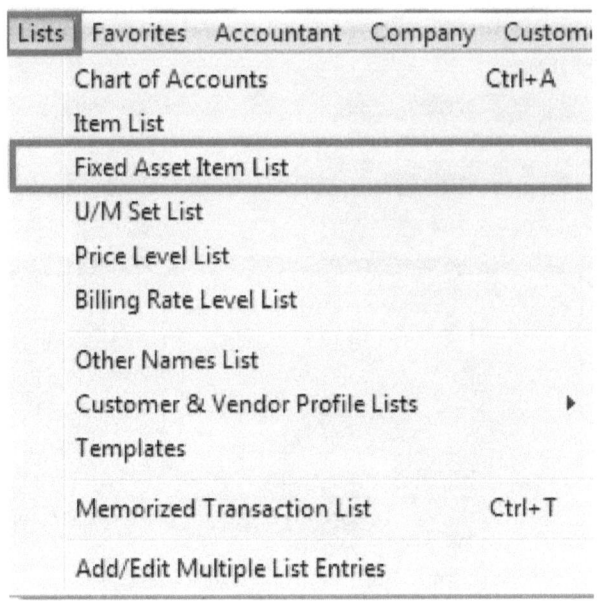

ii. Click Activities at the bottom of the list and click Create Invoices

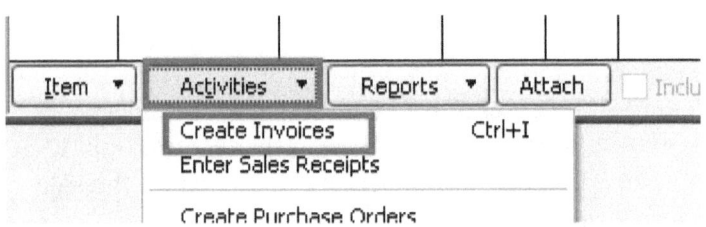

If prompted for help on choosing a sales form, click No.

iii. Enter the Customer:Job and the date

iv. In the Item column, display the Items list and select the asset that you want to sell

v. In the Amount column, enter the asset's sale price

vi. Choose Save & Close

vii. At the prompt about entering more information, click Yes. The Edit Fixed Asset Item window is displayed

viii. Mark the asset as sold

x. Mark the asset as inactive

Record the sale with a general journal entry

Before you enter the sale of the fixed asset:

i. Go to the Company menu and click Make General Journal Entries
ii. Click the Account drop-down list and choose the fixed asset account or subaccount where you track the cost or starting value of the asset
iii. In the Credit field, enter the cost or starting value if you track depreciation in a separate asset account. Otherwise, enter the current book value of the asset as obtained from the QuickReport
iv. In the Name field, enter the name of the asset
v. If you track accumulated depreciation in a separate subaccount, fill in a second line
vi. Enter the selling price on the next line
vii. Enter the net gain or loss on the next line
viii. Save the entry

Currency				☐ Home Currency Adjustment			
Date	11/26/2015	Exchange Rate 1 KES =	1	KES	Entry No. 12		

Account	Debit (KES)	Credit (KES)	Memo	Name	Billable?
Machinery:Cost		500,000.00			
Machinery:Depre...	25,000.00				
Co-operative ban...	495,000.00				
Profit on machinery		20,000.00			

Handling Pre-Paid Expenses

This is an expense paid in advance and has to be expensed over one or more months in the future. This must be recorded properly and in a timely manner. Expense must be recorded in the accounting period in which it is incurred and not in accounting period in which it is paid.

The normal method of making this entry is to use a journal entry. As an example, let's use an annual insurance premium of 48,000. The premium is paid in total in December, and expensed monthly starting January. Upon payment credit bank account and debit the prepaid expenses account (other current asset) with 48,000.

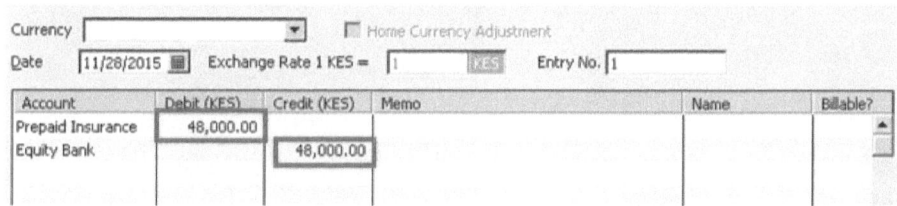

The prepaid expense will be recognized as an expense in the next accounting period starting from January (4000).

Now create a journal entry crediting prepaid expense (4000) and debiting insurance expense account (4,000). This entry debits Insurance expense, increasing the balance by 4,000 to recognize the amount of insurance used up in each month and credits Prepaid insurance to reduce the amount by the same amount. Memorize the monthly transaction (click Edit menu and choose memorize general journal) and use it twelve times in the memorized transaction list.

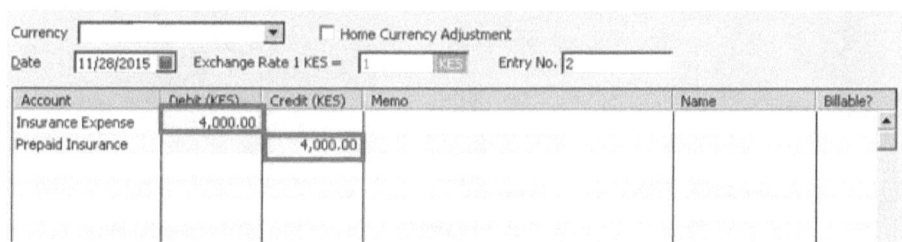

When all journal entries are made immediately and accurately, the total balance of the prepaid expense account should be zero and appear as such on the chart of accounts list. This means every prepaid expense has been accurately entered and expensed over time.

Sales tax

If a business collects sales tax, one must pay it to a tax agency on a regular set up. QuickBooks helps automate your sales tax tracking so one can keep accurate records about the sales taxes collected and paid.

QuickBooks uses sales tax codes to track the taxable or non-taxable status of both the items you sell and your customers. If your tax agency requires you to report the reasons why particular sales are taxable or non-taxable, the sales tax codes that you assign to your items and customers allow you to run reports that provide this information for your sales tax return.

When you turn on sales tax, QuickBooks creates two sales tax codes for you:

a. Use the taxable code i.e. 'TAX' for items and customers that are taxed

b. Use the non-taxable code i.e. 'ON' for items and customers that are not taxed. Non-taxable sales tax codes are also used for some out-of-state sales

These two preset sales tax codes are the only ones needed for many businesses. You can add additional sales tax codes to accommodate other reasons for charging or not charging sales tax on your transactions. Then assign the appropriate sales tax code to each of the products and services you sell, and to each of your customers.

A customer's sales tax code always overrides an item's sales tax code. If you are selling a taxable item to a non-profit customer, the item would not be taxed.

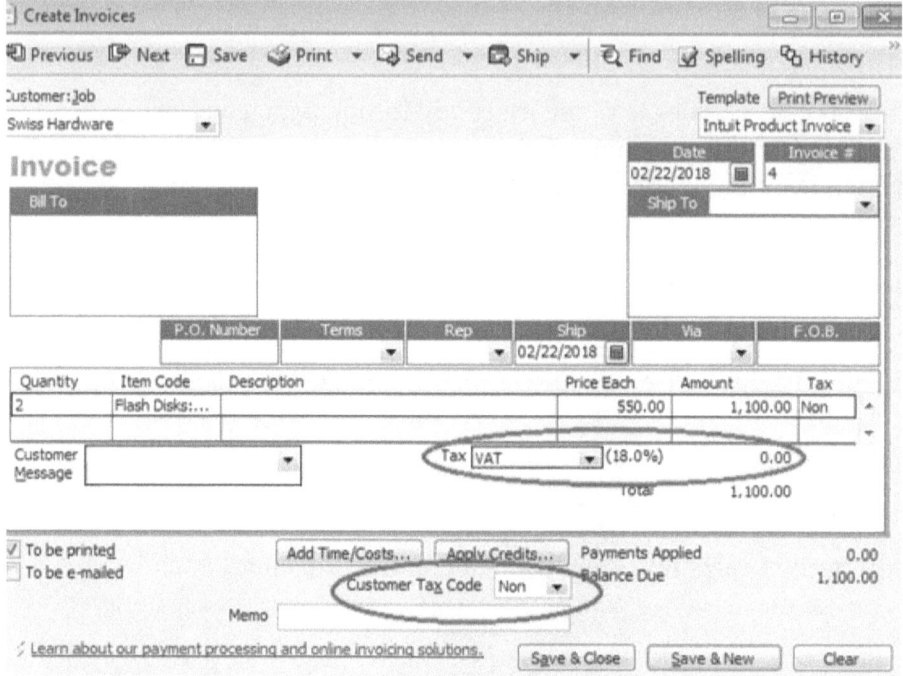

Use sales tax items and rates to charge sales tax

QuickBooks uses **sales tax items** to calculate and add sales tax charges when you make a taxable sale. When you set up a sales tax item, you assign it a sales tax rate and associate it with the tax agency to which you pay the sales tax. Once you've set up sales tax, QuickBooks automatically applies the appropriate sales tax item and rate to the sale of your taxable items. Taxable status of items and customers is determined by the sales tax codes assigned to them. If an item is taxable, and the customer buying that item is taxable, then the sales tax charge is applied to the sale. All of the sales tax items you set up can be found in your Item List.

◆Creative A520			Inventory Part	Sales Account	0	0	5,800.00
◆USB Small speakers			Inventory Part	Sales Account	0	0	350.00
◆TFT Screens			Inventory Part	Sales Account	0	0	0.00
◆15 Inch			Inventory Part	Sales Account	0	0	4,500.00
◆17 Inch			Inventory Part	Sales Account	0	0	5,500.00
◆19 Inch			Inventory Part	Sales Account	0	0	6,500.00
◆20 Inch			Inventory Part	Sales Account	0	0	8,400.00
◆22 Inch			Inventory Part	Sales Account	0	0	10,000.00
◆Bad Debts			Other Charge	Bad Debt			0.00
◆Customs	Sales Tax		Sales Tax Item	Sales Tax Payable			30.0%
◆T	Sales Tax		Sales Tax Item	Sales Tax Payable			14.0%
◆V	Sales Tax		Sales Tax Item	Sales Tax Payable			24.0%
◆VAT	Sales Tax		Sales Tax Item	Sales Tax Payable			18.0%
◆Withholding	Sales Tax		Sales Tax Item	Sales Tax Payable			20.0%

Before you start setting up your sales tax items note:

a. Applicable sales tax rates for the area in which you sell

b. Tax agency to which you pay the collected sales tax

QuickBooks sales tax terminology
a. Tax district

A town, city, county, or state that charges sales tax

b. Tax agency

The government office that sets the obligations for sales tax collection and payment. Tax agencies are set up as vendors, because you make payments to them. Sometimes a tax agency is called a tax authority

c. Sales tax code
The identifier that QuickBooks uses to track the taxable and non-taxable status of items, and the customers to whom you sell these items. For example, a customer that is a non-profit organization would have a non-taxable status. You would not charge sales tax for anything you sell to this particular customer. You can see all of your sales tax codes in the Sales Tax Codes List

```
Sales Tax Item Listing
Modify Report...  Memorize...  Print...  E-mail  Export...  Hide Header  Refresh  Sort By Default
11:54 AM                                    Pson
02/22/18                          Sales Tax Item Listing
                                    February 22, 2018
     Type              Item           Tax Agency        Description      Price
  Sales Tax Item    Customs           KRA               Sales Tax         30.0%
  Sales Tax Item    T                 KRA               Sales Tax         14.0%
  Sales Tax Item    V                 KRA               Sales Tax         24.0%
  Sales Tax Item    VAT               KRA               Sales Tax         16.0%
  Sales Tax Item    Withholding       KRA               Sales Tax         20.0%
```

d. **Sales tax item**

A QuickBooks item that is used to calculate the appropriate sales tax for a sale. A sales tax item includes a sales tax rate and a tax agency. When you sell taxable items, you charge the appropriate sales tax rate by assigning a sales tax item to each sale.

e. **Sales tax rate**

The percentage charged for sales tax by the tax district. For each different district/rate combination, you need to set up a new sales tax item. For example, you may sell in three counties that all charge the same sales tax rate, but you need a separate sales tax item for each county, even though the sales tax rate is the same. This allows you to track the amounts of sales tax you collect for each tax district.

f. **Sales tax group item**

A QuickBooks item that groups multiple sales tax items so you can charge only one rate on your sales. For example, the location where you sell may require you to charge both a county and a state sales tax. However, customers are used to seeing one sales tax rate on sales. You would set up a sales tax group item that combines those two sales tax rates, say 3% for the county and 8% for the state, to create a single, sales tax group item with a rate of 11%. You would apply this sales tax group item to your taxable sales for that county. A sale tax group item also allows you to track the separate sales tax rates on your reports so that you can pay the appropriate amounts to the appropriate tax agencies.

Set up sales tax
Sales tax items, rates, and tax agencies

Understand sales tax items and rates and the difference between a single sales tax and a sales tax group item, because, in some scenarios tax is charged for more than one tax district. One can set up both your single sales tax items and your sales tax group items.

If you're paying multiple agencies, create a sales tax group only.

To set up a sales tax item and rate

a. Open the sales tax preferences

b. In the Sales Tax Preferences window, click the Add sales tax item button

    The New Item window opens with Sales Tax Item already selected in the Type drop-down list.

c. Enter a sales tax name

    Provide a name that describes the location for the tax. The name appears as one of the options in the Tax field on your sales forms.

d. Enter a description for the way this sales tax item will appear as a line item on your sales forms

The description prints on your sales forms after the final line item. You can't edit it on the forms. It's advisable to use the name of the sales tax item as the description.

e. Enter the sales tax rate

   The percentage you enter is the rate you charge when a sale is taxable. E.g. 10%. This rate also appears on your sales forms.

f. In the Tax Agency drop-down list, click Add New

   This will open the New Vendor window one can set up the tax agency (a vendor) to which you pay sales tax.

g. In the Vendor Name field, enter the name of your tax agency. Other information such as the address can be entered later

h. Click OK to close the New Vendor window

i. Click OK to close the New Item window

j. Repeat steps above for each sales tax item you need to set up

k. When you're finished setting up all of your sales tax items, you set up your sales tax group items

l. After setting up all of your sales tax items, click the Most common sales tax drop-down list again and choose the sales tax item that you use most frequently. This choice will be used as the default sales tax item and rate on all of your sales forms. This can be changed for any particular sale

m. You'll be prompted to assign a taxable sales tax code if you already set up your items and customers. If most of your items and customers are taxable, click OK. If most of your items or customers aren't taxable, clear the appropriate checkboxes and then click OK. You can change the sales tax code for those items and customers that don't match the setting you chose later

Sales tax codes

Default sales tax codes will be used to track the taxable and non-taxable sales of your products and services.

The preset taxable "TAX" and non-taxable "NON" sales tax codes you find may be the only ones needed. After you're finished with this setup, you'll assign these sales tax codes to your customers and the items you sell.

If you require specifying additional sales tax codes to track taxable and non-taxable sales, it is recommended that you set them up now but you can set them up later.

Setting up additional sales tax codes

a. In the Sales Tax Preferences window, click the Taxable item code or Non-Taxable item code drop-down list and then click <Add New>

b. In the New Sales Tax Code window, enter a 3-digit sales tax code you want to add and a description for it

c. Click OK

d. Repeat above steps for each sales tax code you need to set up

e. After setting up all your sales tax codes, click the Taxable item code and Non-Taxable item code drop-down lists again and choose a default sales tax code to use

Sales tax payment schedule

This is information about when you need to pay your tax agency. In the Sales Tax Preferences window, in the When do you owe sales tax? section, select when you owe your sales tax to the tax agency, as specified by the tax agency.

a. In the When do you pay sales tax? section, select how often you need to make your sales tax payments to the tax agency, as specified by the tax agency

 Quickbooks sets reminders to pay your sales taxes depending on the time interval you select.

b. Click OK to apply the preferences

Enter an opening balance for sales tax liability

If you collect sales tax and you've set it up, you need to enter an opening balance for your Sales Tax Liability account. After your start date, your sales tax is included on your sales forms and entered into this account.

Do not use this procedure if you entered historical invoices or sales receipts dated before your QuickBooks start date because sales tax will already be included on them and posted to this account. Also skip this procedure if you entered an opening balance for each tax agency as you set it up.

To do this task:

a. Go to Chart of Accounts

b. In the Name column, double-click Sales Tax Payable

If Sales Tax Payable isn't in the list, then you haven't set up the account.

c. fill in the details for the tax agency owed in a blank transaction at the bottom of the register:

   i. Enter your QuickBooks start date field

   ii. Select the tax agency in the Vendor field

   iii. Enter the amount you owed as of your start date in the Billed field

   iv. Select Opening Bal Equity from the Account drop-down list

d. Click Record

e. Repeat the above steps for each tax agency to which you owed sales tax as of your QuickBooks start date

Applying sales tax when you make a sale

QuickBooks automatically charges and calculates sales tax on invoices, sales receipts, estimates, and other sales forms. The sales tax code is the one you assigned to the item for tracking its taxable status

The Tax field, shown at the bottom of the line items, shows the sales tax item or sales tax group item you assigned to the customer. The sales tax rate associated with that sales tax item is shown to the right, in parentheses. QuickBooks uses this sales tax rate to calculate the sales tax

The Customer Tax Code, at the bottom of the sales form, indicates the taxable status you assigned to the particular customer. When making sale, QuickBooks checks your records to see if the customer is taxable. If so, the line items are checked. All taxable line items on the sale are totaled and multiplied by the rate of the sales tax item (or sales tax group item) you assigned to the customer. For Quick Added a new customer, QuickBooks uses the most common sales tax rate that you set up in your sales tax preferences

Pay sales tax
Use the Pay Sales Tax window to create the payment. It shows how much sales tax you currently owe for each sales tax item you use and any sales tax adjustments you've entered and need to apply to your payments.

Paying your sales tax using the Write Checks or Pay Bills windows will cause errors in your bookkeeping and in your sales tax reports.

To do this task:

i. Go to the Vendors menu, choose Sales Tax, and then click Pay Sales Tax

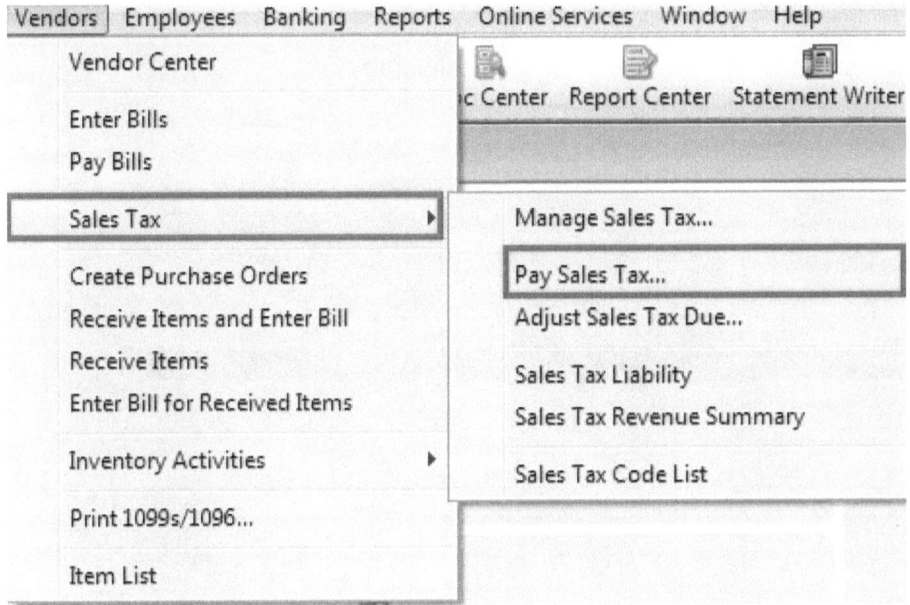

ii. Choose the account you want to use for these tax payments

iii. Check the date shown in the Show sales tax due through field

iv. In the Starting Check No. field, verify that the check number matches the next check that you want to use. If not, change it

v. The list of payments shows all sales taxes that your company owes and any adjustments you've made. For each sales tax item, the list shows the tax agency to which the sales tax is payable and the amount due as of the date shown above. Select the sales tax agencies you want to pay

vi. If you want to make a partial payment to a tax agency, click in the Amt. Paid column and edit the amount

vii. Click OK

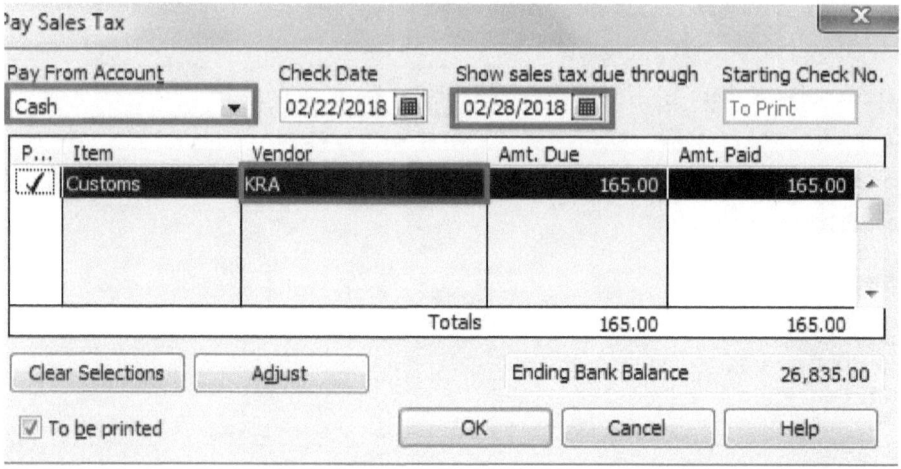

Manufacturing Firm Inventory

The assembly components are deducted from inventory quantities when the new inventory assembly item is created.

a. From Lists choose Item List. QuickBooks displays the item list window

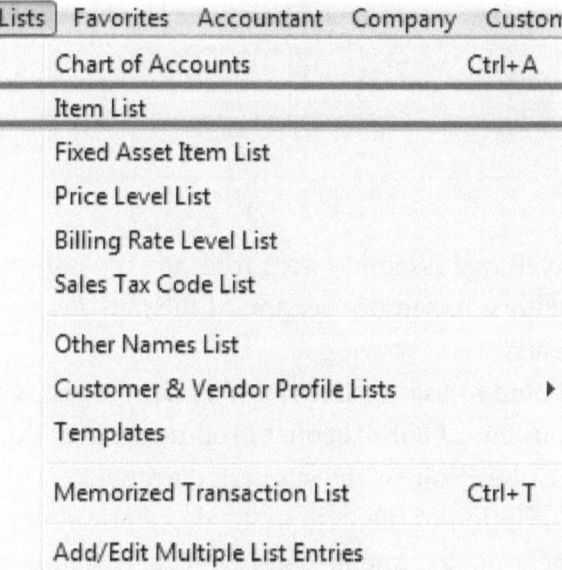

b. Click on item button and then select New from the drop-down list that appears. The new item window appears

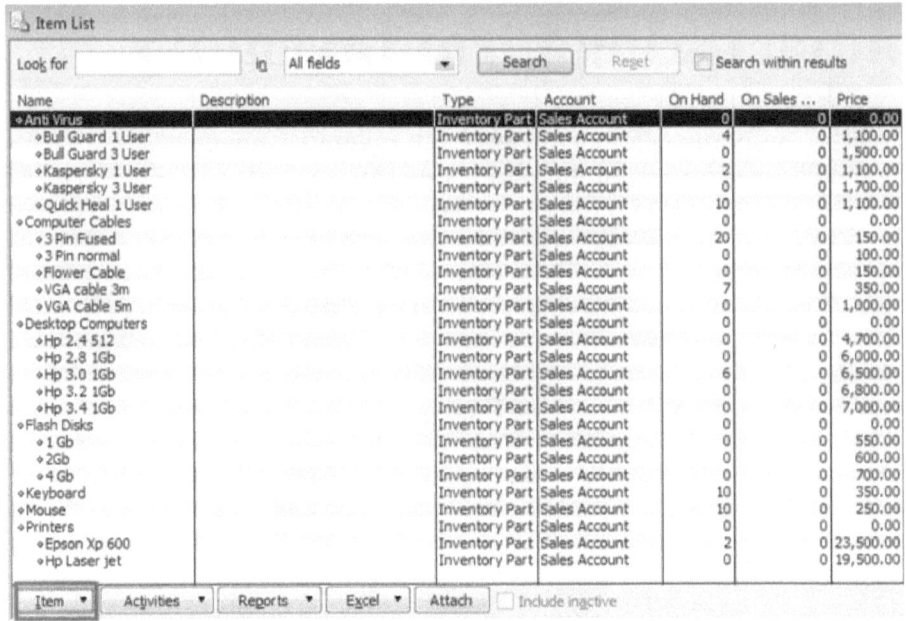

c. Select the Inventory assembly item from the type drop-down list. The Inventory Assembly version of the new item window appears

d. Select an account to use for tracking this item's cost when you sell it from the COGS Account drop-down list. You will find Cost of Goods Sold as the suggested account

e. Type the description of the item in the description text box. This will appear on documents e.g. Invoices, Receipts etc

f. Enter the amount that you charge for the item into sales price box. On the Tax Code drop-down, indicate whether the item is subject to sales tax

g. From the Income Account drop-down list, select the income account to track the income from the sale of the item

h. Identify the individual component items and the quantities needed the make the inventory assembly under the components needed list. Each of these items goes on a separate in the list

i. From the Asset Account drop-down list, specify the Asset account for tracking this inventory item's value, on Build Point text box give the lowest quantity of this item that should remain before more is manufactured, ignore On Hand value and enter current date

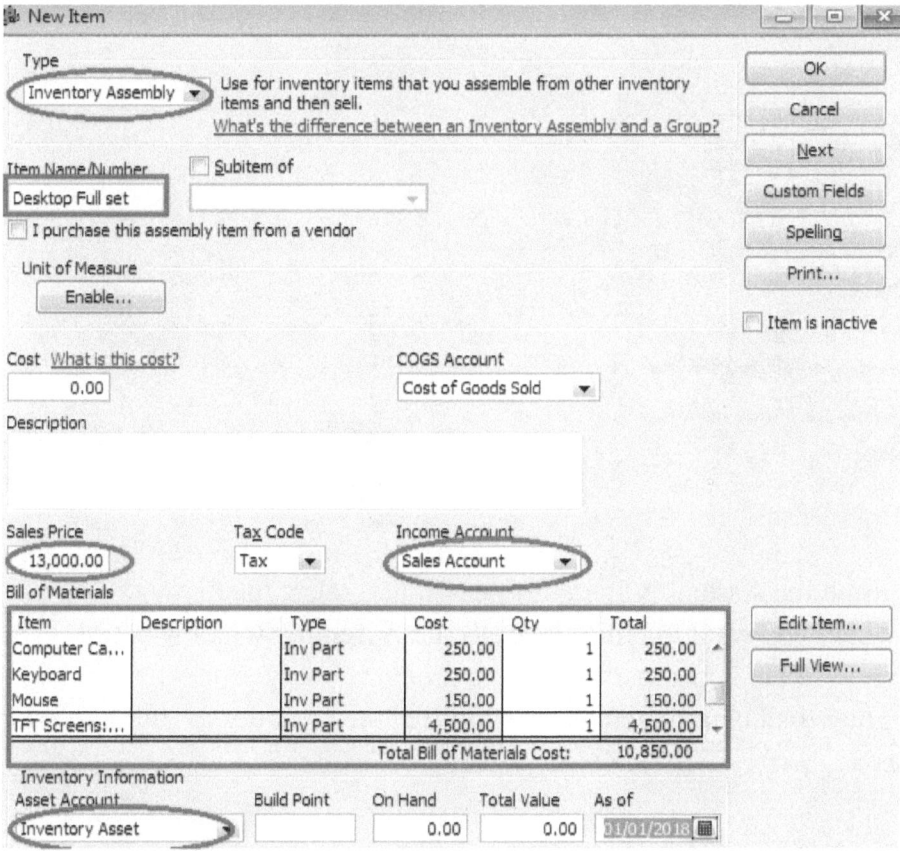

j. Click Ok to save the information. The new item appears under the item list

k. To build the assembly item, choose Vendors, Inventory Activities, Build Assembly. This brings Build Assemblies Window

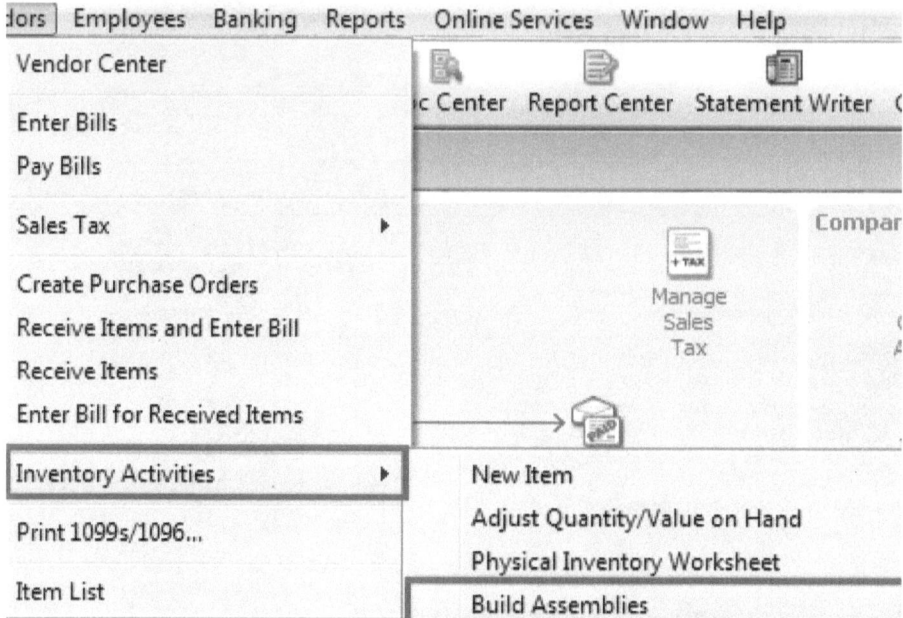

l. From the Assembly Item drop-down list, select the item which you want to build. In the Build Assembly window you will see the items that go into the product
m. Enter the quantity you want to build in the Quantity to Build box

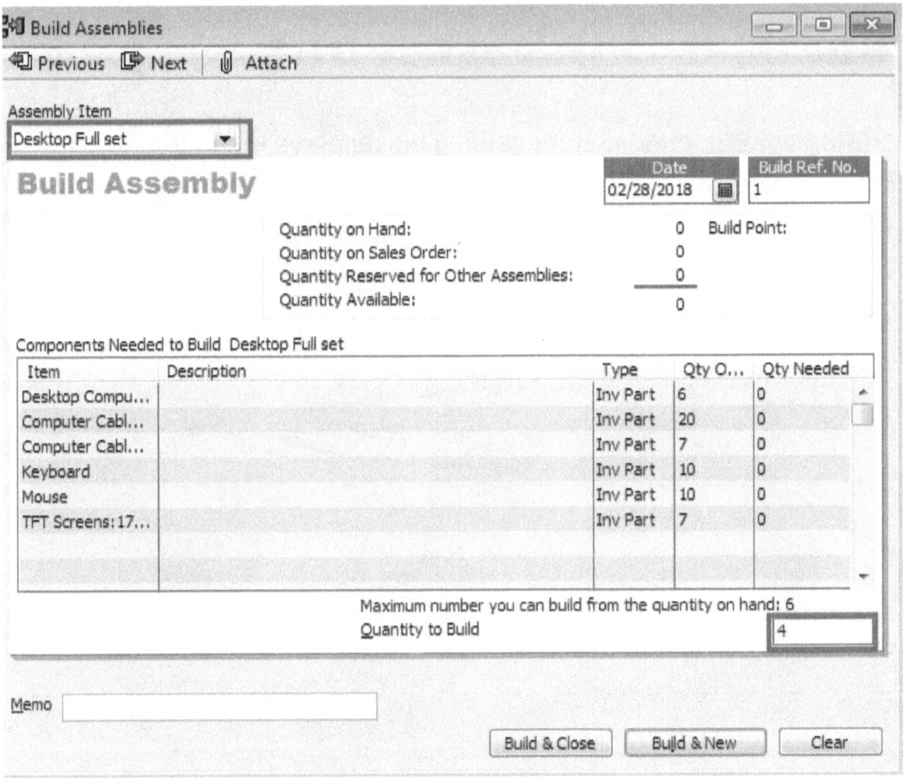

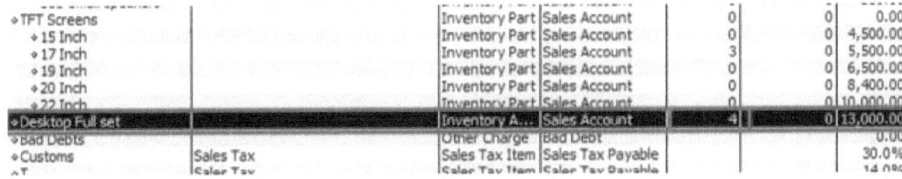

n. Click Build & Close or Build & New

Note that after building an item, the items numbers are affected, that is the assembled item count increases while the number of the items used to build reduces.

Reconcile a Bank Account

a. From banking, choose Reconcile. This displays the begin reconciliation dialog box

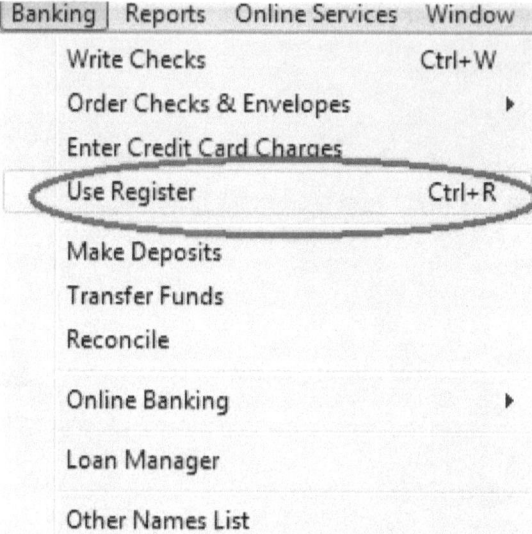

b. Select the account from the account drop-down list
c. Confirm that the beginning balance on the reconcile screen is the same as the beginning balance on your bank statement
d. In the statement date text box, enter the date of the statement

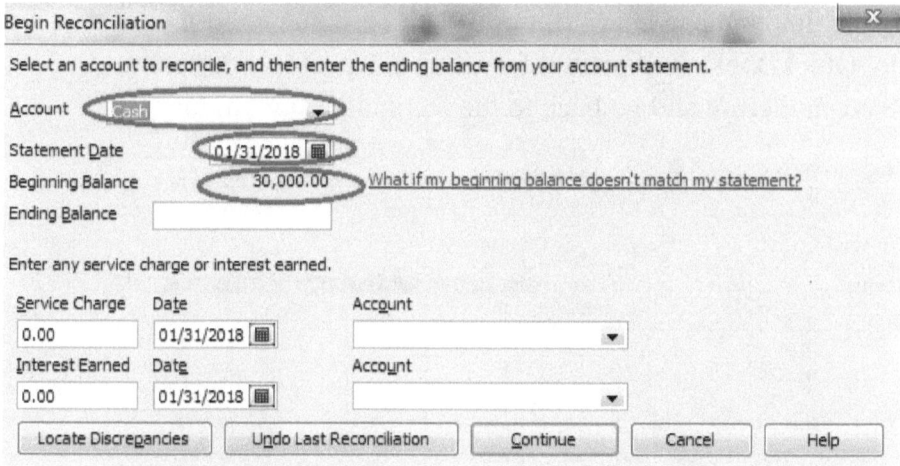

e. Enter the ending balance on the bank statement in the ending balance text box

f. In the service charge and interest earned text boxes, enter the amount if applicable, the date of the transaction and the account that you use to track the service charge and the interest

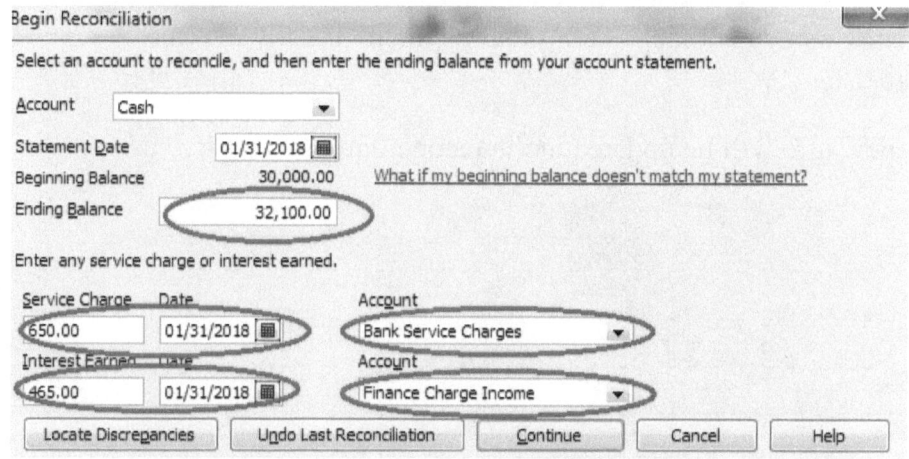

g. Confirming from the bank statement, check off each of the deposits in the "deposits and other credits column"

h. Again, in the "checks and payments" column, check off each of the checks and payments

i. Note that to change any amount, click on it and choose Go to. QuickBooks will open it for editing. Update the amount, Save and close and go back to the reconciliation window

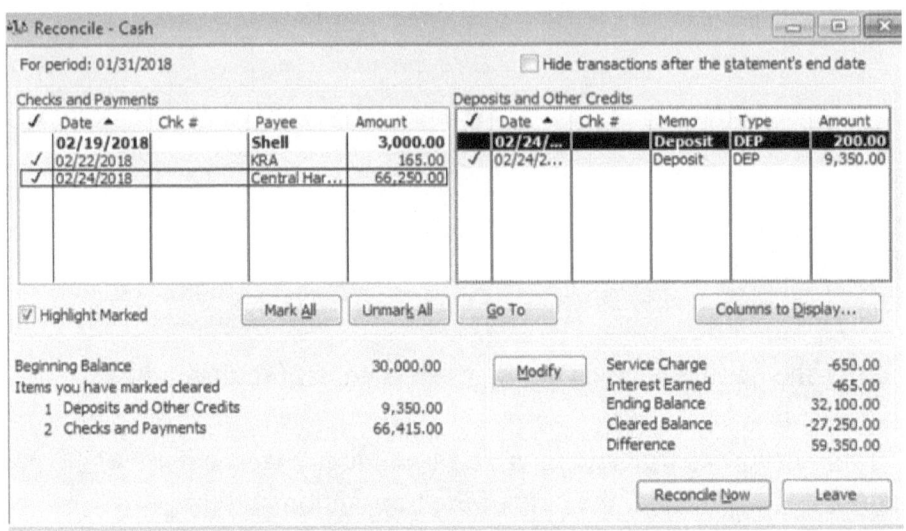

j. To add an item that is missing from your records, go back to the banking menu and click on "Use Register". Here you can enter a payment, deposit or other payment directly into the register

The new info will be updated in the reconciliation window.

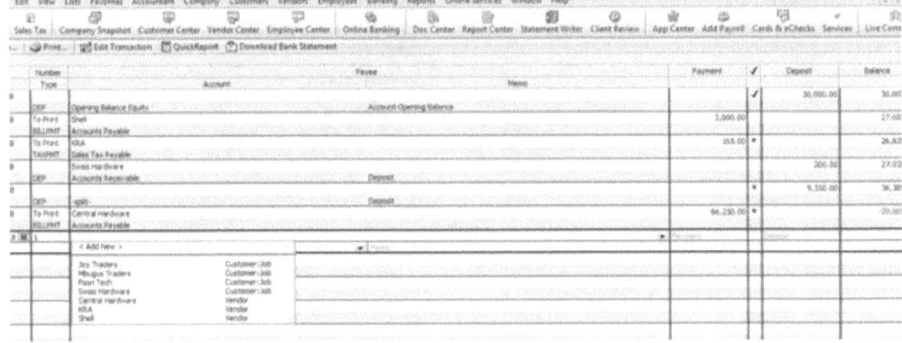

When recording a deposit or a payment, remember to specify an account to indicate what the amount was used for e.g. Account payable for payment and Account receivable for deposit.

2/24/2018	To Print	Central Hardware			66,250.00	✓
	BILLPMT	Accounts Payable				
12/27/2018		Jex Traders		0.00	2500	
		Accounts Receivable		Memo		

In case any item has more than one component, click on the <Splits> button in the check register, this will allow the items to be entered individually.

After all items have been checked off and all missing records included, the difference amount will be zero. Click Reconcile Now button. QuickBooks records the cleared transactions as cleared and redisplays the register window.

By clicking the Leave button QuickBooks saves the half completed reconciliation where one can come back later and finish the reconciliation.

Adding Users in QuickBooks and Giving Them Access

Note that only the QuickBooks Administrator can add users and give them access.

a. Go to the Company menu, choose Set Up Users and Passwords, and then click Set Up Users

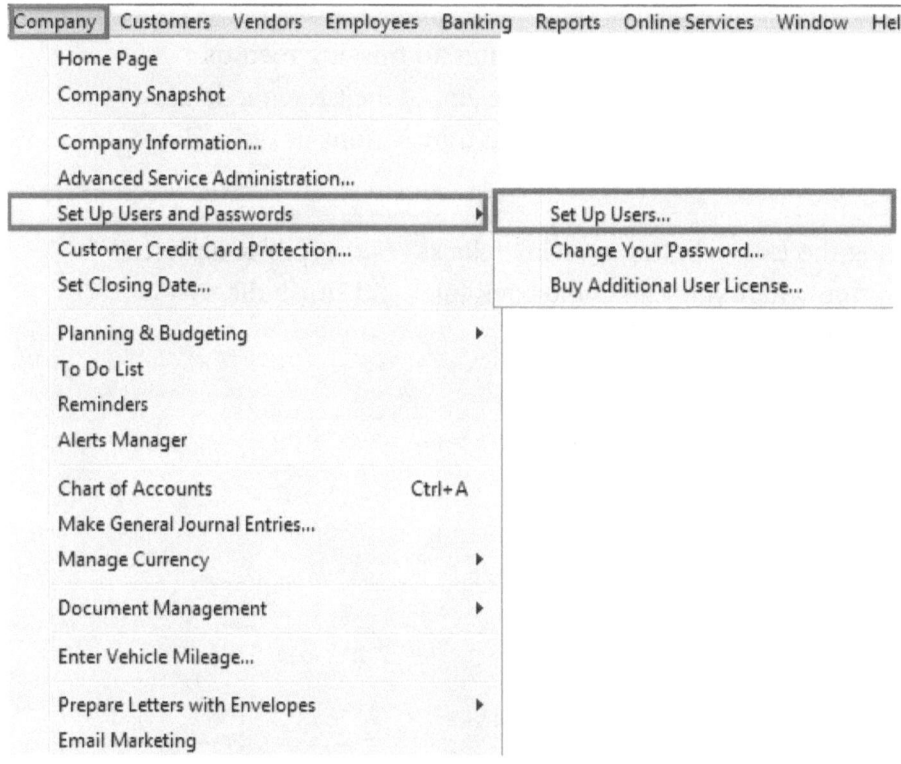

b. Click Add User

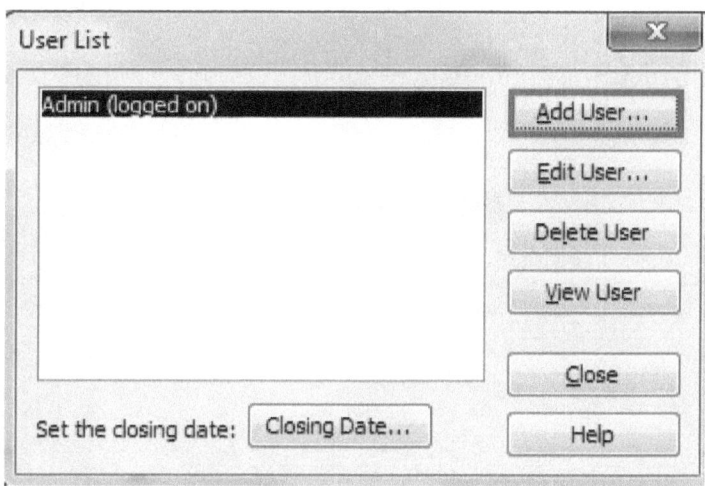

c. Enter the Username of the user in the User Name field

d. Enter a password in the Password field and repeat the password in the Confirm Password field

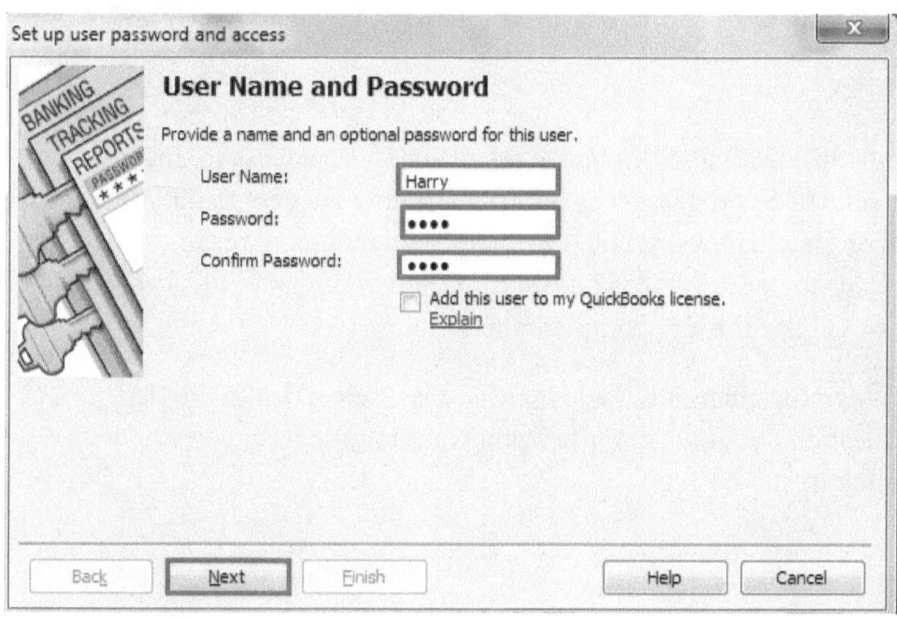

e. Click Next to finish adding the new user

f. Choose whether this person will have access to selected areas of QuickBooks or all areas of QuickBooks

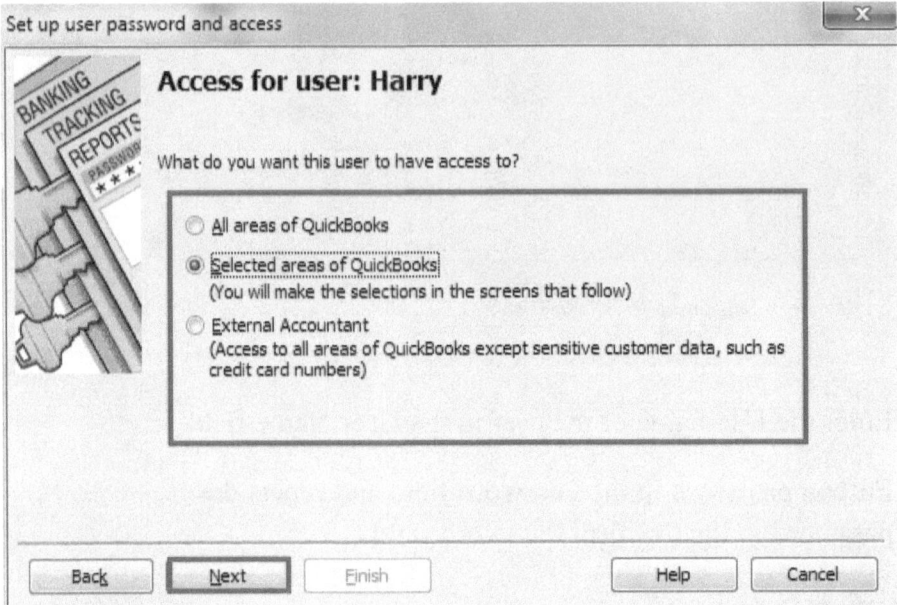

g. Click Next

If you are selecting thelimited areas the user has access to, make your selections on next steps but if you granted access to all areas of QuickBooks, you have no more selections to make. ClickYes to confirm that you want this person to have full access. Click Finish to complete the setup process

h. When the changing the level of access, selectYes to the first question about the activities you want to give to the user and click next

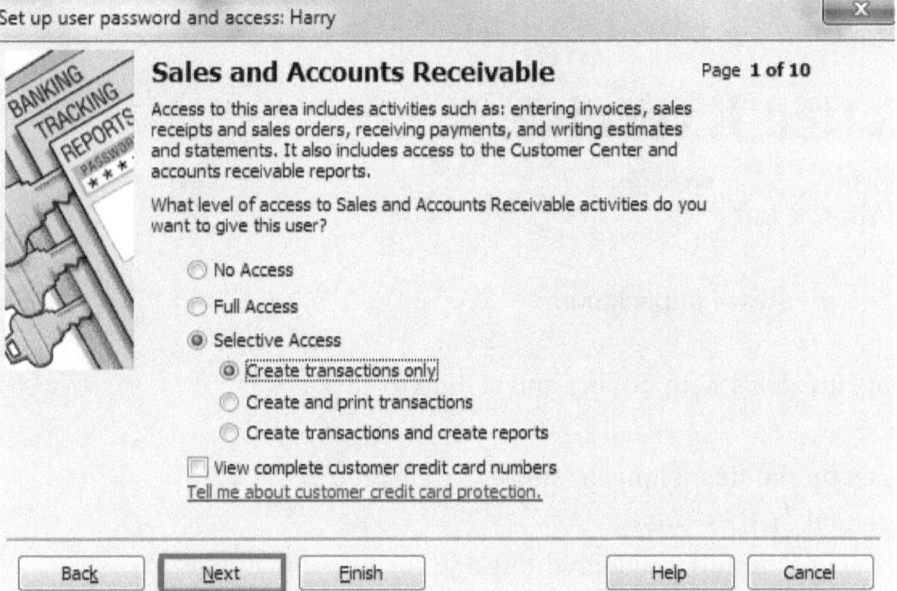

Repeat the above step until you give the access level to all areas.

i. After the last step, review the table that summarizes the access rights you granted to the user. To make a change, click Prev button to return to the appropriate screen

j. Click Finish to complete the User setup process

Practice Exercise

Suwon Allpack Ltd
Tel 855112
Website: www.suwonallpack.com

The Company deals with buying and selling of sacks bags.

a) Set up the financial year starting 1st March 2017, with capital of 1,587,000
b) Record the following creditors and their opening balances as of 1st March 2017
    i. Soil packs 250 000
    ii. Maximum Technologies 51,000
    iii. Mombasa packs Company 50,000
    iv. Betty packers Ltd 25,000
    v. Eden pack 10,000
c) Record the following debtors and their opening balances as on 1st March 2017
    i. Marine company Ltd 800,000
    ii. Uchumi Ltd 250,000
    iii. Kaline Company 60,000
    iv. Allion Company 20,000
    v. Laico packers 12,000
    vi. Mavuno Ltd 120,000
d) Record the following fixed assets:
    i. Pick up cost 250,000; depreciation 5,000
    ii. Computer equipment 100,000; depreciation 2,500
    iii. Furniture 200,000; depreciation 10,000
e) Record Barclays bank account 370,000; Petty cash 50000

f) Pre paid electricity 1,500
g) Record the following Items

Item	Cost Price	Sales Price	On hand
Maize sack	350	480	25
Cement bag	250	320	30
Tea bag	140	240	20
Paper bag	120	170	18

h) Record the following transactions:
i. March 2nd: Company ordered 80 sacks, 50 cement bags from Eden pack packers and 45 paper bags from Soil packs. They were delivered the same day. A transport fee of 1,500 was included
ii. March 3rd: The company bought the following fixed assets; 5 plastic chairs @ 250 and a microwave @ 3500 from Maximum Technologies and cleared the balance using a cheque
iii. March 15th: Uchumi ltd ordered 50 sacks which were sold on credit
iv. March 20th: Marine Company bought 45 tea bags and paid half of the amount which was deposited that day
v. March 22nd: Uchumi ltd returned 6 sacks which were spoilt
vi. March 23rd: Received a water bill from City water company of 1500
vii. March 25th: Received the balances from Uchumi ltd and Marine invoices using cheque and deposited.
viii. March 28th: The cheque which was received from Marine bounced. The charged Marine a penalty of 2%
ix. April 2nd: Paid a bill received from City Water Company on 23rd using a cheque

x.	April 5th: Received a cheque from Marine for the bounced cheque plus the penalty
xi.	April 6th: The company invoiced Uchumi and Allion for sale of 20 tea bags and 40 paper bags respectively plus 16% VAT
xii.	April 7th: Laico, Uchumi and Allion paid half of their opening balances
xiii.	April 9th: Marine company cleared their opening balances
xiv.	April 15th: The Company bought 100 cement bags. A discount of 5% was given. Paid the same day by cheque.
xv.	April 17th: Record the pickup depreciation of 3,500
xvi.	April 18th: The Company bought 50 cement bags, 60 maize sacks and 80 paper bags from Betty packers and were delivered the same day. A discount of 1.5% was given
xvii.	April 19th: Marine Company bought 100 cement bags. A transport fee of 2,500 was included. They paid on the spot
xviii.	April 20th: The company paid for the goods received on April 18th
xix.	April 21st: A computer worth 25,000 was bought and paid through Petty cash
xx.	April 22nd: The company detergents from Tuskys ltd worth 1,200 and paid using petty cash
xxi.	April 25th: Fire broke out and 10 cement bags and 5 tea bags were destroyed
xxii.	April 27th: Neema bought on credit 40 maize sacks and 70 paper bags
xxiii.	April 28th: Transferred 25,000 from barclays bank to petty cash
xxiv.	April 30th: Received electricity bill from worth 1,500

xxv. May 2nd: Allion collapsed and their balances were written off

xxvi. May 6th: You memorized the invoice that you wrote on April 27th for future use. Save it as "neemainv"

xxvii. May 10th: Disposed the pickup with an original cost of 250,000 and accumulated depreciation at a disposal cost of 275,000

xxviii. May 16th: Jose Ltd bought 45 cement bags on credit. A discount of 1.5% was offered

xxix. May 20th: You used the memorized invoice neemainv to sell goods as it is to the same customer

xxx. May 24th: Acquired a loan from cooperative bank worth 200,000 and was spent as follows:
- a) 100,000 used to buy a motor bike
- b) 50,000 to buy BAT shares
- c) 30,000 deposited to co operative bank account
- d) 20,000 deposited to petty cash account

xxxi. May 25th: All debtors cleared their balances

xxxii. June 2nd: Paid a quarter of the loan using Barclays account

xxxiii. June 5th: Received 10,000 a donation from Adelaide packs

xxxiv. June 10th: Cleared all balances owed to suppliers

www.ingramcontent.com/pod-product-compliance
Lightning Source LLC
Chambersburg PA
CBHW031421210526
45464CB00005B/1990